THE POWER OF A POSITIVE ATTITUDE

THE POWER OF
A POSITIVE ATTITUDE

DISCOVERING THE KEY TO SUCCESS

Roger Fritz

AMERICAN MANAGEMENT ASSOCIATION
New York • Atlanta • Brussels • Chicago • Mexico City • San Francisco
Shanghai • Tokyo • Toronto • Washington, D.C.

Special discounts on bulk quantities of AMACOM books are available to corporations, professional associations, and other organizations. For details, contact Special Sales Department, AMACOM, a division of American Management Association, 1601 Broadway, New York, NY 10019.
Tel.: 212-903-8316. Fax: 212-903-8083.
Website: www. amacombooks.org

This publication is designed to provide accurate and authoritative information in regard to the subject matter covered. It is sold with the understanding that the publisher is not engaged in rendering legal, accounting, or other professional service. If legal advice or other expert assistance is required, the services of a competent professional person should be sought.

Library of Congress Cataloging-in-Publication Data

Fritz, Roger.
   The power of a positive attitude: discovering the key to success / Roger Fritz.
     p.   cm.
   Includes bibliographical references and index.
   ISBN-13: 978-0-8144-1013-4
   ISBN-10: 0-8144-1013-8
   1. Employees—Attitudes.   2. Attitude (Psychology)   3. Success.   I. Title.

  HF5549.5.M63F75   2008
  650.1—dc22

                        2007047262

Published under license from JMW Group, Inc.
One West Ave., Larchmont, New York 10538.

Printing number
10 9 8 7 6 5 4 3 2 1

CONTENTS

When the Armstrong Electronics Co., opened their new plant, Al Armstrong, the founder and president, hired Steve M. to supervise days and Gary J. to lead the night shift.

They came to him with excellent credentials. Both had degrees in electrical engineering; both had supervised manufacturing units in electronic companies and met the technical standards needed for the position.

Why did it happen that one year later Gary's night shift consistently outperformed Steve's day group? Not only did the day crew fail to meet standards for quantity and quality of production, it also had a high rate of absenteeism and turnover. Some of the employees had filed grievances with the union about unfair treatment. The night shift had an enviable production record, little absenteeism or turnover, and not a single grievance had been filed.

Al discussed this situation with Roger Fritz, an internationally acclaimed consultant, and the author of this book. After interviewing both men and observing them on the job, Fritz gave this report: "The answer in one word," he said, "*attitude*." He then elaborated: "Gary's positive attitude inspired his people to face obstacles and work hard to overcome them. When confronted with similar problems, Steve came up with arbitrary solutions (which often didn't work), and his people were not motivated to extend themselves to find better answers." Fritz then developed a practical plan to help Steve change his attitude and at the same time reinforce Gary's positive outlook.

Attitude involves not only how we see the world around us, but also how we interpret situations, circumstances, and the actions of others. In other words, if your outlook is to be meaningful, it must take into account how others react to it. A positive attitude without interaction is meaningless.

Steve and Gary may have been equal in their technical competence, but the attitude they brought to the job made the difference between Gary's success and Steve's failure.

Many people are not really aware of the true nature of the attitude with which they approach many phases of their lives. They are so accustomed to behaving in the same ways, they don't realize the root causes of their successes or failure.

In this book, you will develop a better understanding of the effects of your attitude. Equally important, it will help you see more clearly how a positive attitude influences not only your performance but also results achieved by others around you.

Why is this important? Three reasons: First, because attitude affects how you look, what you say, and what you do. Second, because it affects how you feel, both physically and mentally. And third, it affects how successful you are in achieving your goals. What could be more basic?

Your attitude stems from within. If you think you can change it from negative to positive, you have taken the first step to do so. You have the capacity to control your thoughts. The world makes way only for people who are determined, for people who laugh at barriers that limit others, at stumbling-blocks over which others fall.

Building a positive attitude begins with having confidence in yourself. Confidence reinforces ability, doubles energy, buttresses mental faculties, and increases power. Your thoughts will prompt the force of your conviction, the weight of your decision, and the power of your confidence.

The constant affirmation of your ability to succeed, and your determination to do so, will carry you past difficulties and strengthen your power to achieve; it will enable you to defy obstacles and laugh at misfortunes. It will reinforce your natural faculties and powers and keeps them on track.

Constant affirmation increases courage, and courage is the

backbone of confidence. Furthermore, when people like Gary, when in a tight place say "I must," "I can," "I will," they not only reinforce their courage and strengthen their confidence, but also weaken the opposite qualities. Whatever strengthens a positive will weaken the corresponding negative.

If we analyze great achievements and the people who accomplished them, the most prominent quality in evidence is a positive attitude. People with absolute faith that they will do what they undertake are the most likely to succeed, even when such an attitude seems to outsiders audacious, if not foolhardy.

The practice of positive thinking increases ability tremendously, for two reasons. First, because it uncovers talents that before were locked up, then calls out hitherto unknown resources; and second, it keeps the mind in focus by curtailing fear, worry, and anxiety, all enemies of success. It puts the mind in a condition to succeed. It sharpens the perceptions and makes them keener. It gives you a renewal source. It turns you about so that you face toward your goal, toward certainty, toward confidence and assurance, instead of doubt, fear, and uncertainty. It helps you capitalize on the results of your efforts instead of allowing extra caution or worry to neutralize future effort.

• • •

The author of this book, Roger Fritz, is president of Organization Development Consultants, located in Naperville, Illinois. He has over forty years of experience as an educator (University of Wisconsin and Purdue), manager (Cummins Engine), corporate executive (John Deere), university president (Willamette University), and highly successful consultant to clients, including AT&T, Brunswick, IBM, Caterpillar, State Farm Insurance, Motorola, Pizza Hut, Sara Lee, as well as over 350 other corporations and organizations, large and small, throughout the world.

Dr. Fritz has written fifty books, produced twenty-five audio albums, and edited three video training series. Six corporations have tapped his broad experience as a member of their Board of Directors. His columns in weekly newspapers and monthly national magazines reach millions of readers providing a continuing influence on how Americans increase their effectiveness on and off their job. His books are published and distributed in thirty-eight countries and languages.

Just as he has helped so many clients overcome negatives and reinforce their positive attitudes, his ideas and suggestions will help you in many ways for a long time.

Maintaining a positive attitude uncovers hidden abilities and calls up untapped resources. It frames the conditions needed to make the best use of talents—provide fresh outlooks—set goals with confidence, and overcome reluctance to trying new things.

As you read this book, think of how each of the principles examined can have a positive effect on your personal life and career as you apply them day-to-day.

Arthur R. Pell, Ph.D., *Editor*

CHAPTER 1

INTERPRETING YOUR WORLD

"Any fact facing us is not as important as our attitude toward it, for that determines our success or failure."
—NORMAN VINCENT PEALE

The first step to developing a positive attitude is to become aware of the true nature of your current attitude. This isn't always as easy as it sounds, but how you react to various situations can reveal a great deal about your basic attitude. To succeed in any of your endeavors you must approach them with a positive or affirmative attitude.

YOUR POSITIVE ATTITUDE QUOTIENT (PAQ)

To determine your PAQ—Positive Attitude Quotient—use the following ten questions to decide how frequently you exhibit that particular behavior. Mark 1 if never, 2 if seldom, 3 if sometimes, 4 if usually, and 5 if almost always. Remember, this is to help determine your Positive Attitude Quotient, so be honest with yourself. When you have finished taking the test, add up the numbers you assigned to each item.

_____ I can quickly recover from failure.

_____ I have personal goals I am working on.

_____ I keep track of my progress on goals and make the changes needed.

_____ I make up my mind slowly whether or not I will like new people I meet.

_____ I get a lot of good ideas from other people.

_____ I can find what I need to know without much help.

_____ I don't have to be reminded to do what I agree to do.

_____ I can quickly detect people who are pessimists.

_____ I enjoy listening to people's explanations, even if I don't like them personally.

_____ I am patient with people who disagree with me.

Total: _____

Let's discuss the implications of your total score.

If you scored 40 or more, you have a strong positive attitude. This will provide credibility as a leader and compatibility as a coworker.

If you scored between 30 and 40, you have a normal positive attitude. It will serve you well and be a favorable influence on others.

If you scored between 20 and 30, your attitude is unpredictable and will cause confusion and uncertainty in your relationships at home and at work.

If you scored under 20, you have a negative attitude, which will inhibit confidence in your relationships and work.

Using the PAQ scale will help you decide which of these areas to work on to increase your positive attitude and influence.

[ASSESS YOUR ATTITUDE TOWARD YOURSELF]

If you are physically well, the quality of your life will depend mostly on your attitude. It's important, therefore, to consider that attitude reflects both inwardly on yourself and outwardly to other people.

Ask yourself these questions to determine if you usually take a positive attitude toward yourself. Answer Yes/No/Undecided.

1. Are you a learner or rejecter? Are you usually willing to recognize that no one has all the answers, and continue trying?

2. Do you do your best on-the-job? Evidence of this would be if you tend to suggest better ways of doing things.

3. Do you demonstrate enthusiasm in most of what you say and do? What does the record say about that? What will your friends tell you?

4. Are you willing to grow? Do you think it's your responsibility to prepare yourself for advancement, or wait for someone else to tell you what to do?

5. Do you welcome changes? Are you the kind of person who experiments, who tries things, who is generally open to suggestions?

6. And last, but certainly not least, do you cultivate a sense of humor? Do you take yourself more seriously than anyone else? Do you get some joy out of what you're doing at work? Is it fun for you?

[EVALUATE YOUR ATTITUDE TOWARD OTHER PEOPLE]

"Attitude is a little thing that makes a big difference."
—WINSTON CHURCHILL

Are you taking a consistently positive attitude toward other people? Here are some ways you can check this out.

Are you sincerely *interested?* Do you talk about their needs and their problems? Sincerity can't be faked.

Do you look at others' point of view? How they feel, why they feel that way, why they think and act as they do? Do you study them? Are a good listener?

Are you able to cooperate to achieve common goals? Are you a good team player?

[ATTITUDE REFLECTS POSITIVELY AND NEGATIVELY]

Attitude affects every aspect of your life and your job. A good example is safety in the workplace. A negative attitude can lead to:

- *Carelessness.* "It doesn't really matter."
- *Ignorance.* "I didn't know that would explode."
- *Fatalism.* "If it happens, it happens."
- *Cynicism.* "All these films and posters are just kid's stuff."
- *Laziness.* "It's too much trouble to wear that hard hat or eye guard or those protective shoes."
- *Recklessness.* "Danger is the spice of life." Or, "I like to live on the edge."

- *Overconfidence.* "I haven't been hurt in twenty years; it's not liable to happen now."

On the other hand, a positive attitude leads to:

- *Planning ahead.* "It may take a little longer, but I'd rather do it the right way and be safe."

- *Encouraging others.* "I want to know what your goals are, because I want us both to improve."

- *Showing appreciation.* "Thanks for that suggestion."

- *Thoroughness.* "I want to do it right the first time so nobody gets hurt here."

- *Conscientiousness.* "I want to fix this now so I don't forget and it might be a hazard to someone."

- *Alertness.* "If I concentrate and am careful now, it'll be safer for everybody concerned."

Success requires more than talent. While talent and knowledge are essential, the key that unlocks them both is your state of mind. Being positive makes you more dependable. . . . When you are positive you will find that you instinctively respect others, and are therefore more considerate. You will have pride in your own work, and you will give credit to others where it is due. You will help them do their job more efficiently where possible and you will share your enthusiasm with those around you. Even a smile will transmit encouragement to others—and this will be picked up and fed back to you.

Recognize that the enemy is usually within and that the first step in analyzing attitude is to start with yourself.

[MAKE UP YOUR MIND TO BE POSITIVE]

*"All human beings can alter their lives
by altering their attitudes."*
—ANDREW CARNEGIE

Learn to find pleasure in simple things. Make the best of your circumstances. No one has everything, and everyone has something of sorrow intermingled with the gladness in their life. The trick is to make the laughter outweigh the tears. Don't try to avoid all risks. Don't think that somehow you should be protected from misfortunes that befall others. That's not liable to happen, and you'll be disappointed when you find out that it doesn't. The future is always uncertain.

You can't please everybody. Don't let criticism overly influence you. Don't let your neighbors or "conventional wisdom" make decisions for you. Be yourself. It will work out better in the long run. Do the things that you enjoy doing. Don't borrow trouble. Imaginary things are often harder to bear than reality.

"Hate poisons the soul," said Robert Louis Stevenson, so don't envy what other people have. Don't hold grudges. Avoid people who make you unhappy. Have many interests. If you can't travel, read about new places. Don't regret where you haven't been, or what you haven't done. Don't hold post mortems. Don't spend your life brooding over sorrows and mistakes.

Don't be the one who never gets over things. Stop and think about the people in your life who live in the past or are holding grudges. Consider their attitude, whether it's positive or negative, and whether you want to be like them.

Do what you can do for those less fortunate than yourself. And above all, keep busy at something, or several things. A busy person doesn't have time to be unhappy.

When you get to a point where your present situation is leading to a lot of self-doubt, remember, life is a journey not a destination. We are always in the process of arriving at conclusions. That's because we are always struggling with change or fear or failure or even success. Yes, success can create problems too, and we will discuss some. Adjustments are always needed.

First-time experiences are often risky. You must adjust to new circumstances. You may have to adapt to different people. You have to decide how much emotion you should show, particularly at work. You can worry about whether you are in a rut, and if so, how to get out of it. To cope with new experiences, a positive self-image and a positive attitude are invaluable.

There is powerful evidence of how self-image influences results. The way you see yourself affects your attitude, which in turn affects your actions, which determine your accomplishments.

The key, then, for gaining confidence, earning respect, and effecting positive change with better results, lies in developing and maintaining a good self-image. The sad news is that most of us often fall short because we don't do the daily self-image maintenance necessary. The underlying problem is that we are drifting and reacting rather than initiating action. Think of it as planting a crop. If we want a better crop of self-worth, confidence, opportunities, we must change and gain control of what can be done, not worry about what cannot be done. If you're a farmer, you can't worry about the weather constantly.

We deserve more than to waste time and energy blaming others for bad breaks, indulging in self-pity, seeking revenge, or focusing on past mistakes. We've got to understand our doubts and fears. But change doesn't simply come from analysis. It only comes from action. It's never easy and requires determination and discipline.

[CHANGE THE WAY YOU FEEL ABOUT YOURSELF]

"The only disability in life is a bad attitude."
—SCOTT HAMILTON

You *can* change the way you feel about yourself. These suggestions will help:

1. *Cast away your negative past.* List your personal liabilities, past mistakes, failures, and embarrassments. Burn it. Watch it turned to ashes and say aloud, "That's the last time I will let you get me down. I have more important things to do." Your actions always reinforce your dominant thoughts. Learn from those past bloopers and get rid of them. Get them off your back. There are enough monkeys in this world waiting to jump on it for you.

2. *Evaluate your attributes.* List your personal assets, competencies, and achievements. A realistic résumé is a good start. Ask your friends for help. Read it aloud three times a day for three weeks, and then read it as soon as you get up each day thereafter. Your actions reinforce your dominant thoughts. If you have ever felt valuable, worthy, or good in the past, you can feel that way again. You spent many years allowing others to program you. Now it's up to you.

3. *Seek out positive input.* Read or listen to something motivational or inspirational everyday. Positive imagery requires positive examples. You also need other people's experiences. Their research, techniques, and results can cut years off your learning curve and save you from painful trial and error.

4. *Write down specific goals.* This triggers your inborn, automatic goal-seeking mechanism. Even while you sleep, your subconscious will help you overcome roadblocks, obstacles, and defeats. As you achieve your goals, the written proof sup-

ports you as a worthy, achieving person, and plants good self-image seeds.

5. *Take responsibility for your emotional environment.* It's hard to soar like an eagle when you are surrounded by a bunch of turkeys. The law of emotional gravity is strong. You become like those with whom you associate.

These beginning self-image building steps may seem simplistic, but they are based on sound research and results. They are the foundation for a strong—what I call *internal*—net worth. When you believe in and support your strengths and values and accept responsibility for being a deserving, creating achiever, then and only then, will you have moved toward being a positive influence on other people.

[PULL YOURSELF UP]

"Those who keep trying can renew themselves."

Expecting lasting success to come quickly is foolish. Most often, it involves starting at the bottom of the ladder and working your way up, rung by rung. The case of baseball great Eddie Matthews is a good example.

After graduating from high school in Santa Barbara, California, seventeen-year-old Matthews received two offers to play professional baseball. One came from the Brooklyn Dodgers and included a $60,000 signing bonus. The other came from the Boston Braves (now the Atlanta Braves) and carried a $4,000 bonus.

Matthews weighed the two options. If he went with the Dodgers, he would get more money and immediately be on the roster of a big league team. If he went with the Braves, he would get less money and be expected to start out on one of their minor league teams.

Matthews realized that he had a great deal to learn. He felt that starting in the minor leagues would be the best way to get experience and accepted the Braves' contract. It was a wise decision.

In the minors, Matthews played with and against many former major league stars whose careers were winding down. By hanging around with them on and off the field, he learned the key ingredients to success: play hard every day, be humble, and do whatever it takes to win.

During his career, Matthews hit 512 home runs, tying Ernie Banks for thirteenth on the all-time career home run list. He hit thirty or more home runs in nine straight seasons (a record), forty or more home runs *four times*, played in ten All Star games, and was inducted into the National Baseball Hall of Fame in 1978.

Research verifies Matthews' decision. A recent study at the University of Minnesota concluded that young people who have part-time jobs in their teens have an advantage later in life. The reasons can be traced to lessons they learned involving time, budgeting, money management, interpersonal skills, and handling work stress.

What can we conclude? That those who learn early have more "staying power" than those who must rush to become qualified later on.

[REWORK MISTAKES]

Most people believe that Richard Wagner became a world famous composer because he was gifted. True, he liked theater, art, and music, but he disliked being on stage, could draw nothing more complex than stick figures, and was a slow learner on the piano. But lack of talent was overcome by great determination.

When he dreamed of becoming a composer at the age of fifteen, he headed for the library, checked out a book on the subject, and memorized it. To train his ear, he asked a violinist from the Leipzig Orchestra to teach him about chords and keys, learning the technique of every orchestral instrument but the harp. He studied the works of successful composers including Beethoven to understand how to capture a sound.

Still, Wagner's early compositions were terrible. His first audience couldn't stop laughing. Embarrassed, the seventeen-year-old sneaked out of the theater.

To see what he had been doing wrong, Wagner sought the opinion of a local church musician. He was told to get a better understanding of the basics before setting out to try something new. He began to go over the works of Bach and Mozart line by line until he could construct a lyrical phrase.

Given a second chance, the audience liked his work and his career was on its way. Open to ideas from anywhere, Wagner once sat at a piano to write some music after lunch. Downstairs, a neighbor began to hammer on a sheet of tin, creating a terrible clamor. Instead of stopping or leaving, he concentrated on the noise and began to make his music blend with the racket. That piece became part of a major scene in Wagner's famous opera *Siegfried*.

Philip Knight, the founder of Nike, is convinced that the work needed to grow his business was far more rewarding than running a big company day to day, so he turned that job over to someone else. Bill Gates and Donald Dell did the same. Steve Jobs waited too late at Apple Computer, was ousted by shareholders, but returned later determined to take the company to new heights . . . and he did.

[LOOK FOR A BETTER WAY]

When you have the right attitude, you can find great success even when you are confronted with failure or obstacles.

Chester Carlson used the pain from arthritis in his hands to motivate him to develop a machine that *Fortune* magazine once called "the most successful product in history."

Responsibility came early to young Chester. By age fourteen he needed to work to support his invalid parents. His mother passed away when he was seventeen and his father when he was twenty-four. The early setbacks made him more determined. He put himself through Cal Tech, earned a degree in physics, and was turned down by eighty-two firms before being hired by Bell Labs in New York. Laid off in 1933 he soon began experimenting with his ideas in the kitchen of his small apartment.

In 1934 Carlson's job was to make copies of drawings by hand. Day after day the pain got worse and he began to work on ways to replace carbon paper and mimeographs.

Finally in October 1938, Carlson and an associate, Otto Kornei, gave birth to the first office copier. His invention was turned down by twenty companies including General Electric, RCA, and IBM before being purchased in 1946 by Haloid, which added Xerox to its name in 1958.

"Hoping and wishing are never enough. Change and improvement come only when determination sparks action."

CHAPTER 2

HOW ATTITUDE AFFECTS RESULTS

*"I am not saying a Positive Attitude can make you successful.
I am saying a Positive Attitude will make you successful."*
—Norman Vincent Peale

Nobody, but nobody is more important to your job satisfaction and happiness, your progress and development on the job than your boss. Some people are lucky to be assigned to a boss who is a good leader, teacher, and mentor, while others may work for one who is the opposite.

No matter who the fates give you as a supervisor, you can make the most of it by studying your boss's goals, style, and work habits and then tailoring your actions accordingly.

Linda learned very early in her assignment to the Purchasing Department that Carol, the purchasing manager, was the kind of person who was meticulous in her work and expected her people to be the same. She observed that Carol was always at her desk ten minutes before starting time, that she organized her work carefully, and that there was a place for everything and everything was in its place. Linda's previous boss had been much more casual, and Linda's work habits when working for him reflected that. She resolved to change her methods of operation. She came in a bit earlier than her boss, set up her desk in a very organized manner, and even dressed more conservatively. This immediately set the stage for a successful relationship with Carol and led to a long, happy employment and rapid advancement.

[DO'S AND DON'TS IN DEALING WITH YOUR BOSS]

Here are some basic guidelines that will help you develop coping strategies for dealing with your supervisor.

The Do's

- DO watch the example of the people who get along with your boss. They, after all, have learned how to cope. Try to learn from them and follow their example.

- DO consider that you may be partly responsible for your poor relationship with your supervisor if you have one. Remember it takes two to tango. And while you can't change your boss, you can change how you behave, so take responsibility and take action to make positive change happen.

- DO try to make your employer's job easier by offering to take responsibility for those tasks that he may dislike doing.

- DO keep track of your boss's mood swings. Observe the times of day and the days of week when he is in the most receptive frame of mind.

- DO tell the boss how you feel about her treatment of you. Don't hide your feelings. Wait until she has cooled down to discuss how you feel, and then talk calmly and, of course, in private.

- DO monitor your progress. If you are not having the success you desire, reevaluate the way you are dealing with your supervisor and take another tack if necessary. Be patient. Don't expect it all to happen at once.

The Don'ts

- DON'T dispute your employer's authority, even if you disagree with her judgment in a particular situation.
- DON'T take criticism as a personal attack. Even if your boss is out of line, it will help to distinguish between your job, which may be bearable, and your boss, who may not be.
- DON'T put yourself in a position to be criticized by seeking the boss' approval when it isn't required. Do some things, and tell him about them . . . later.
- DON'T malign your boss by gossiping behind her back. Be loyal!
- DON'T go over the boss' head unless it's absolutely critical such as an emergency or crisis situation. Violating the chain of command almost always causes more problems than it solves.
- And above all, DON'T lose your self-respect. If your coping strategies have failed and a transfer is impossible, do what you have to do to keep your self-esteem, even if it means finding a new job and a new boss.

"Final judgment about people must be based not on words or intentions, but evidence and results."

[IDENTIFY ACCOUNTABLE PEOPLE]

Most business failure is caused not by lack of money but because of discovering too late that the wrong people have been involved. Consider the people around you—your boss, your colleagues, and your employees—to determine if they are helping you or pulling you down.

The Least Valuable People (LVP) Profile

I developed the profile that follows as a means of identifying the individuals who are now behaving in a way that will likely cause them to fail. I call it my Least Valuable People profile. To my delight, it also identifies the individuals who are most likely to succeed, the people you want to surround yourself with.

This multipurpose checklist is also very easy to use. There are only two answers possible to each issue: Guilty and Not Guilty.

Start by rating yourself first.

	Guilty	Not Guilty
1. Constantly sidesteps problems and complaints, hoping someone else will handle them.	_____	_____
2. Avoids disciplining people.	_____	_____
3. Blames others when things go wrong.	_____	_____
4. Allows false statements to go unchallenged.	_____	_____
5. Doesn't worry about being late for work or meetings.	_____	_____
6. Postpones completion of projects as long as possible.	_____	_____

7. Avoids seeking clarification of misunderstandings in order to criticize later.   _____   _____

8. Never volunteers for an assignment when not absolutely certain of success.   _____   _____

9. Doesn't worry about deadlines.   _____   _____

10. Maintains the same sources of information and bases decisions more on opinions than facts.   _____   _____

11. Tries to be as noncommittal as possible.   _____   _____

12. Punishes good people who disagree.   _____   _____

13. Sees delegating as a way of getting rid of unpleasant chores rather than improving and expanding productivity.   _____   _____

14. Keeps busy on current projects and is uncomfortable about future planning.   _____   _____

15. Allows someone else to do recruiting and selection.   _____   _____

16. Tends to criticize others in public, rather than in private.   _____   _____

17. Is insulated from contact with customers.   _____   _____

18. Frequently talks about how much others depend on them.   _____   _____

19. Is not concerned about nurturing promotable people.   _____   _____

20. Is uncomfortable when depending on others to provide answers.   _____   _____

21. Concentrates efforts on favorite tasks rather than highest priorities.   _____   _____

(continues)

22. Rarely compliments others for their good work.   _____ _____

23. Downplays the competence of other people.   _____ _____

24. Takes as few risks as possible.   _____ _____

25. Waits as long as possible before delivering
bad news.   _____ _____

26. Limits efforts to "on-the-job" hours; rarely
takes work home.   _____ _____

27. Is not involved in self-improvement programs.   _____ _____

28. Joins in conversations about the "good old days"
as often as possible.   _____ _____

29. Talks a lot about how difficult it is to objectively
measure what they do.   _____ _____

30. Hides talented people to further their own career.   _____ _____

Now take the opportunity to analyze the results of your responses:

0–4 Guilty verdicts: This is the accountable person you need most. Don't let them get away.

5–10 Guilty verdicts: This person is likely to qualify for greater responsibility with proper coaching and management. Be prepared to mentor them

11–20 Guilty verdicts: This person is making you more vulnerable every day—watch them carefully.

More than 20 Guilty verdicts: This person is likely to seriously handicap you. If you are his supervisor, you may want to start keeping written records of problem areas and discuss it with a friend in Human Resources.

If you are a coworker, stay as far away as possible. If he is your supervisor, well, maintain a positive attitude, stay polite—and try to get a transfer.

[GET THE HELP YOU NEED]

"Keep away from people who try to belittle your ambitions. Small people always do that, but the really great make you feel that you too can become great."
—MARK TWAIN

Successful people acknowledge that they are vulnerable in their dependence upon the performance of others. They also realize they can *benefit* by choosing to be around people who will enhance their own capabilities whether they are your staff, your colleagues, or your mentors and bosses.

Using the LVP profile, you can learn to avoid problem situations before they get worse. The profile will also help identify the potential of those who:

- *Go above and beyond expectations.* They don't stop when they've achieved what others have done before them.

- *Bring solutions, not more problems.* Their track record indicates that they never say: "You have a problem," but rather: "*We* have a problem. Let me see if I can give you some recommendations to solve it."

- *Bounce back from mistakes.* They do not blame others for their own errors. They rarely say, "I did what you told me and it was wrong." They are resilient and find new ways to do things.

- *Don't make excuses.* If things go wrong, they admit and go on to fix the problem.

- *Don't depend on reminders to complete their work.* They are able to set interim deadlines for long-range tasks so they don't panic on the due date.

- *Work for improvement, not perfection.* People who seek perfection in everything they do tend to get frustrated and put themselves under so much pressure that they rarely accomplish what they are capable of doing.

- *Think ahead.* This helps eliminate unpleasant surprises.

- *Don't dwell on successes.* They quickly move on from past accomplishments as well as past mistakes.

- *Don't assume too much.* When in doubt, they ask for clarification.

- *Negotiate agreements and then get going.* They don't wait for orders to be sure they are doing everything *exactly* as it was before.

The people most needed in any organization are initiators, negotiators, and teachers/trainers. If you are finding, hiring, keeping, and seeking to work more with people who are strong in the areas listed above, your chances of success are great.

[WHAT'S WRONG VS. WHO'S WRONG]

Embedded near the surface in this discussion about your responsibility for initiative, as evidence of a positive attitude, is the issue of concentrating consistently on *what* is wrong versus *who* is wrong. Concentrating on who is wrong means that you always try to find someone to blame. When you are surrounded by an aura of trying to find someone to blame, everybody knows about it, and they will all be defensive, waiting for the next shoe to drop.

[ATTITUDE AND EFFECTIVENESS]

*"Success or failure in business is caused more by
mental attitude than by mental capacities."*
—Sir Walter Scott

Unfortunately we overlook the relationship between attitude and effectiveness. Your effectiveness, especially if you are a supervisor or manager or in any kind of a leadership position, is judged in large part by how your attitude has influenced the results achieved. Here are some of the questions you should be asking yourself.

- What is the *factual* evidence that you really want people who report to you to succeed?

- What is the evidence that you allocate an adequate amount of time to plan with them? To think ahead? Provide needed resources?

- What is the evidence that you'll be calm in a crisis or emergency when others are behaving irrationally? Losing your cool or having a temper tantrum will affect how they react to you.

- What is the evidence that you encourage calculated risk, but avoid shooting the messengers of bad news? If that's the way you consistently behave, it's going to be pretty tough to find people willing to be messengers.

- What is the evidence that you can disagree without being disagreeable?

- What is the evidence that you do not flaunt the symbols of status and power and privilege, which may yield fear, isolation, and suspicion?

- What is the evidence that you negotiate objectives to make them stretching, yet realistic and attainable? Can you negotiate rather than order? Can you coach rather than direct?

- What is the evidence that you are rarely surprised, and can quickly find out what you need to know? It's not important that you know everything that you need to know exactly when it's needed, but it's absolutely essential that surprises be minimized and you know where to get pertinent information.

- What is the evidence that you can simplify rather than complicate issues? Are you usually understood? How often do people come back to you and say, "I didn't understand that. What did you really mean?"

- What is the evidence that you will encourage dissenting points of view to arrive at a better decision? It is said that when Alfred Sloan, the legendary chairman of the General Motors board of directors, counted a unanimous vote on a subject he would say, "I'm uneasy with that conclusion. We will adjourn and reconvene in the morning. There must be more to this than we currently see."

If you can't provide clear answers to these questions, the people who are in a position to move your career forward may also not have adequate evidence of how your attitudes contribute to the organization. Make sure that your attitudes are clearly present in your day-to-day behavior and actions.

[OVERCOMING YOUR OWN NEGATIVE ATTITUDES]

"The greatest discovery of my generation is that a human being can alter their life by altering attitudes."
—WILLIAM JAMES

There will be times when you must come to the realization that you, yourself, are the problem. When this happens, these tips will help:

1. Put your negative attitudes in focus. "If I keep this up, where will it lead?"

2. Laugh. There's no question that laughter is good medicine.

3. Accept setbacks and failures as part of life, but keep in mind that a positive attitude may lessen the length and severity of problems.

4. Talk calmly to yourself when you are upset. This can greatly lower your stress level. Take time to unwind. Have lunch away from your work on a stressful day to recharge.

5. Talk positively to yourself when you feel down.

6. Examine your priorities and goals. Are they yours or the expectations of others?

7. Simplify everything you can.

8. Don't let small problems get bigger.

9. Get more involved with family and friends. Keep close ties with people who enhance life's good times and to buffer the bad. Try to put as much thought and energy into making your relationships work as you put into your job.

10. Brainstorm positive alternatives with others. What could have been said or done to indicate a more positive or constructive approach?

Most of this will not come easily. It's never easy to apologize, to begin over, to admit errors, to keep trying, to take advice. It's never easy to face a sneer. It's certainly not easy to avoid mistakes, because we know some are inevitable.

Surprisingly, it's not easy to sustain success. Too many temptations are difficult to cope with. It's not easy to break a bad habit, keep out of a rut, or to forgive and forget.

It's not easy to think before we act. It's not easy to subdue an unruly temper. And it's not easy to shoulder blame, even though it's deserved.

None of these things are easy, but they all lead to better days.

[BUILD UP YOUR SELF-CONFIDENCE]

"If you have a positive attitude and constantly strive to give your best effort, eventually you will overcome your immediate problems and find you are ready for greater challenges."
— PAT RILEY

How can you learn to believe in yourself? This is the core of confidence. Attitude shows many things, but one of its most important and prominent reflections is your confidence.

Two important issues to tackle to increase your self-confidence are: (1) knowing your limitations and (2) learning to make choices.

What Limitations Will You Accept?

In the 1960s, Jimmy Heuga was one of the top skiers in the world. He won a bronze medal in the 1964 Olympic slalom but in 1968, at age twenty-five, to his disappointment, he only placed eighth in that event. He was unaware that he was developing multiple sclerosis. When his disease was diagnosed, several doctors said that nerve damage was so severe he had to be confined to a wheelchair. He refused to believe them. Despite his condition, he made a practice of riding his bicycle to work, exercising, and swimming for twenty minutes every day. He even taught himself to ski all over again.

His view was that he could tolerate being in a wheelchair, but could not tolerate waiting around helplessly. His goal was to reanimate his life through a health program. His philosophy is simple: the key, he believed, is to work around the disease. For example, if you don't know how to swim, you don't jump into the lake. First you may get your feet wet, then each day you wade a little deeper until you gain the confidence to swim. This attitude not only helped Heuga cope with his illness, but also inspired him to establish the Heuga Center, which provides programs based on his own experience to help other people with MS (for details go to www.heuga.org).

Powerful advice for anyone, isn't it?

What Choices Do You Make?

"Choice is uncomfortable, because it makes us feel responsible," says Ann Weber, an Asheville, North Carolina, psychologist. "The advantage of indecision is being blameless, but the disadvantage is a life out of [your own] control," she says.

Jane Burka, a psychologist from Berkeley, California, identifies several types of indecisive personalities. *Perfectionists*, for example, are people who would rather avoid a decision than risk making a mistake. *Non-compromisers* are people who want it all and feel compromised if they have to give up anything. *Freedom lovers* are those who, confronted with several options, don't want to commit themselves to just one. They want their options always open. And *dependents* are people who trust others more than they trust themselves.

Now, the common denominator linking these types is—you guessed it—a lack of self-esteem, which can so often be traced to upbringing. A perfectionist may come from a family in which mistakes were criticized. A dependent could have been told they made bad decisions and finally stopped trying.

San Diego writer Mike Hernacki says his lack of self-confidence and subsequent indecisiveness were rooted in his harsh upbringing, characterized by a puritanical "don't praise, don't brag about your children, don't compliment them" attitude. "I could bring home 10 As and a B and my father would say, 'What's with the B?'"

Hernacki tells how he dated the same woman for four years, but couldn't ask her to marry him until she gave him an ultimatum. He noted that he spent many years bouncing around careers: teacher to advertising executive to lawyer to stockbroker. He finally pursued his fantasy to become a writer, after delaying for fourteen years, because his earlier careers, in his words, "didn't make any money."

When Frank McCourt came to this country from Ireland, he was penniless, unskilled, and friendless. By working menial and tough labor jobs, he managed to finance a college education. Like Hernacki, he wanted to write, but instead became a teacher of English in the New York City high schools. It was only after his retirement that he had the self-confidence to start a writing career. His first book, *Angela's Ashes*, became a best seller and led to two additional best-selling memoirs.

Psychologists Meryle Gillman and Diane Gage, in their book, *The Confidence Quotient: 10 Steps to Conquer Self-Doubt*, advise indecisive people to recognize the negative messages they've received. Then they should visualize a *doubter*, such as the parent who always berated their decisions, and a *reinforcer*, someone who was consistently supportive, and imagine them working together positively. The more decisions you make, and the more you see the world won't fall apart either way, the more control you have.

If you want to be more decisive, start by forcing yourself to make several small decisions every day. Don't wait until you feel in total control. It's like saying, "I'll quit smoking when I don't like the taste." That's never going to happen. You have to decide what steps you will take to accomplish this—and then take them.

Indecisiveness is fear of the future. Once you act, you usually find it's not as horrific as you thought. Start by breaking down decisions into small steps. With personal investments, for example, you don't have to learn about the whole stock market. Just learn what you need to know about the investments you want to make.

Most decisions are less important than your commitment to them, and few are fatal, Hernacki believes. What's important is the willingness to make them work.

"Decision-making still doesn't always come easily," says Hernacki, "but it's different now that I have a history of making decisions. I get out there and make them."

"Positive attitude enables us to focus not on uncontrollable events or circumstances, but on our response to them."

CHAPTER 3

EFFECTIVE LEADERS ARE POSITIVE

"Looking back with regrets is a dangerous and self-defeating habit because it prevents a positive attitude. Move on!"

What people learn from their successes and failures is directly related to their attitude. CEO or mail clerk, or something in between, you would do well to emulate the qualities of those who are successful in a position of leadership.

[CHARACTERISTICS OF SUCCESSFUL LEADERS]

Let's look for a moment at how a positive attitude influences successful leaders.

- They have high frustration tolerance.
- They encourage participation by others.
- They continually question themselves.
- They are cleanly competitive.
- They control impulses to get even.

- They win without exulting.
- They lose without moping.
- They recognize legal, ethical, and moral restrictions.
- They are conscious of group loyalties.
- They have realistic goals.

Regardless of whether you are currently managing a large staff or are just beginning a career, you can learn from successful leaders about what it takes to get to the top. You can see that you have to be realistic about your own personal growth rate. Ask yourself: "Do I wait for someone else, or do I take charge of my own development?" Successful people have no special mandate from The Almighty. Physically, emotionally, even intellectually, they seem very much like most of us. They have varying personalities and intelligence, and their methods of working toward goals are different.

A positive attitude **also ignites the drive to excel in yourself and those around you.** You can stimulate this drive to grow and accomplish when you:

- Implement ideas, whether your own or ideas from others, by harnessing them in practical ways.
- Accept responsibility.
- Make critical decisions with minimal personal agony.
- Emphasize facts over opinions. You should always first gather the facts, and then interpret them when you are solving a problem or seizing an opportunity.
- Be a master of communication. Others will feel free to talk with you because they know that when they have something to say to you, you will be receptive.
- Confirm that others' jobs and ideas are important.

In addition, successful leaders relate well to people. Most people don't fail because of technical incompetence. The major stumbling block is that they simply cannot work effectively with those around them. Those who relate well have learned how to gain genuine respect by:

- Treating people as they would want to be treated
- Becoming good teachers and trainers
- Criticizing constructively
- Controlling their personal desires

These are only some of the many qualities that successful leaders have mastered, and you—no matter where you currently sit on the power ladder at work—can begin to master them as well.

Other characteristics are equally important. You can emulate successful leaders by:

- Explaining carefully when you are introducing something new, anticipate problems, objections, and fears. Look at change from other people's point of view. Try to see what needs to be cleared away so others will cooperate.

- Not being afraid to admit when you don't have all the answers. And your questions should always be directed toward building, solving, revising, and improving, rather than finding out who was at fault or should be blamed.

- Being curious. Successful people are aware and wide-awake when it comes to current events and developments in their field and within the firm. They tend to read more and watch television less. They devote their energy to high priorities and the things that matter most. You can do this too.

- Not being afraid to take risks. Take calculated risks on people, on situations, and in seeking solutions for tough problems. More than sheer courage is involved, however. You will sometimes put your job on the line in testing new or untried ideas.

- Using humor in generating a "let's do it" challenge to which their people—and be sure to include yourself in the challenge—respond. When change is likely to occur, these attributes are worth their weight in gold.

- Rewarding excellence, not mediocrity. This results in greater job satisfaction, motivation, and staff morale by providing ways for employees to participate in achieving their career goals. Even if you are not a manager, you can write e-mails complimenting team members and other employees to their bosses. Kind words and a willingness to go out of your way to point out someone's excellent work can go a long way.

"A positive attitude enables us to make up our minds against stalemates and in favor of progress."

[BELIEVE IN YOURSELF]

The essence of a positive attitude is belief in yourself. In these shifting times, it is virtually impossible to be certain of anything. The only people who are sure of what they think are the inveterate pessimists who say situations can only grow worse. To some extent, this is a self-fulfilling prophecy, because negativism is contagious. To believe something is impossible means that it probably will be.

This little parable, "The Man Who Sold Hot Dogs," probably dates back to the 1930s, but it bears repeating today:

There was a man who lived by the side of the road and sold hot dogs. He was hard of hearing, so he had no radio. He had trouble with his eyes, so he read no newspapers. But he sold good hot dogs. He stood at the side of the road and cried, "Buy a hot dog, Mister!" and people bought. He increased his meat and bun orders. He bought a bigger stove to take care of his trade. He finally got his son home from college to help him out.

Then something happened. His son said, "Dad, haven't you been listening to the radio? Haven't you been reading the newspapers? The European situation is terrible. The domestic situation is worse." Whereupon the father thought, "Well, my son's been to college. He reads the papers and he listens to the radio, and he ought to know." So the father cut down his meat and bun orders. He took down his signs. He no longer bothered to stand out on the highway and sell his hot dogs. And his hot dog sales fell, almost overnight. "You're right, son," said the father to the boy. "We certainly are in the middle of a Great Depression."

With so much gloom hanging in the air, people are unable to see what's ahead of them. They naturally hesitate to move into the unknown. They want reassurance that they will not stumble or fall or break their necks before they commit themselves. In a situation like this, remember what is sometimes called the law of destiny: *glory may be fleeting, but obscurity is forever.*

Uncertainty will stop some people in their tracks, while others will take it in stride as a normal part of living. We can't ask for certainty at any time, because "sure things" don't exist in real life, anymore than they do at the racetrack. There are no certainties, only probabilities. Self-confident people calculate that these probabilities will work in their favor over time.

With this kind of confidence, you don't depend on something or somebody else. You don't depend on the guarantee of security. You depend on yourself and on the things you believe in. You make your own way.

"A happy person is not a person in a certain set of circumstances,
but rather a person with a certain set of attitudes."
—HUGH DOWNS

[THE IMPORTANCE OF HOW WE APPEAR TO OTHERS]

"We awaken in others the same attitude
of mind we hold toward them."
—ELBERT HUBBARD

Self-confidence develops and projects a positive attitude. But sometimes how we feel inside and how we appear to others are very different. Because we are not always aware of how others view us it's vitally important to put their perceptions in balance with our own. For example: Why do some people take themselves so seriously? Why do they get such obvious satisfaction out of displaying their prestige and authority? Sometimes it is insecurity. They are not genuinely confident of their own worth, so seek to reassure themselves by constantly displaying their own superiority and seeking recognition from others.

Vanity is another reason. We all like to feel important but can look silly when our egos are not controlled. To highlight this point, consider putting this note near your workplace. It would read, "Only two groups of people fall for flattery: men and women." It's a good idea once in a while to look around and be sure your feet are on the ground and your head is not too high in the clouds.

Shallowness can cause people to exaggerate their importance and make them see only a tiny part of the picture.

It's not unusual for individuals with a positive attitude to pull ahead of the pack and become leaders. Why? First, their affirmative attitude causes them to deal with problems more effectively. They tend to achieve more on the job, and usually feel more happiness in their personal lives. People tend to respect and follow leaders with positive attitudes. When they have authority, they will use it, but not because they think they are special, superior beings. They use it to get the results desired. They don't believe that being a leader makes others inferior.

There is only one thing more irritating than a young person who takes him- or herself too seriously, and that's an older person who does the same and ought to know better. So if you fall into either category, beware!

[THE CHALLENGE OF LEADING]

Several years ago I worked with a Senior V.P. of a $350 million retail store chain, which hoped to triple sales in five years. I asked him, "What personal development will this rapid growth require of you?" His answer, "I don't think about that. Frankly, I never thought I would get this far. I have a lot of confidence in myself so the future doesn't scare me." He was resisting self-examination and self-assessment. He was not grooming candidates to succeed him. He sealed off his future because he did not, at that lofty position with twenty-five years of experience, understand that change must begin within himself. It was also interesting to note that no one else in the executive group thought he was promotable.

"Ideas are not rare. Making them useful is."

Whenever you're asked to lead, whether it is a small project or a corporate division, the objective is the same: to achieve specific goals through the efforts of others. No matter what methods you select, your major responsibility must be to provide leadership in achieving expected results. Although this may seem relatively simple, the requirements for making it happen are demanding.

[KEY FACTORS INVOLVED IN LEADERSHIP]

To provide an environment in which people can perform at their best, both as individuals and as team members, leaders must:

- Plan carefully, yet be flexible and improvise when the unexpected happens.

- Introduce new ideas and procedures, yet handle the day-to-day chores required to keep the group moving forward.

- Ask the right questions—those that stimulate thinking, initiate action, and foster improvement.

- Check the progress of individuals and groups to make needed changes and determine new courses of action to keep people and plans on target.

- Convince rather than dominate. This requires paying attention to and improving communication skills—listening and responding in words that are easily understood. Instead of imposing your own ideas and preferences, you will be more effective if you persuade and lead by example.

[WHAT EFFECTIVENESS REQUIRES]

"Winners mix optimism with opportunity."

Today's successful competitors are deeply committed to self-development and lifelong learning. They have taken time to study their organizations' structures, policies, and objectives and clearly understand responsibilities as well as lines of authority. They are able to identify group loyalties and relationships, pinpointing growth and development opportunities for themselves and those they supervise.

Effective leadership demands not only continuous learning, but a thorough awareness of trends and emerging patterns. To attempt to stay the same is to fall behind. Leaders who are able to compete successfully:

- Are effective in dealing with people. They keep the organization working purposefully and harmoniously. They approach problems in an orderly way, but with a human touch. They are thoughtful, tactful, and careful. As they strive for improved performance, they consistently maintain the respect of those around them.

- Are self-motivated. They manage themselves and constantly develop their capabilities. They eagerly seek out new ideas and techniques.

- Understand the need for results and effectiveness vs. efficiency. Efficient people do things right. Effective people do the *right* things right.

- Identify key result areas and measures of progress. Split-second decision making is not a requirement. The best competitors think through what must be done, then take the necessary action.

As strange as it may seem, many people don't have a clear-cut picture of what their job requires. Try this short exercise to assess your performance priorities:

Write an answer to this question: "What am I paid to accomplish?" Use no more than four words per item. Avoid directional indicators like "increase" and "satisfy." Avoid quantities and timings when listing key objectives. Limit your list to eight items.

Test your results by evaluating the items against these criteria:

- Do they represent output, rather than input?
- Are they an important part of your position?
- Do they fall within the active limits of your authority and responsibility?
- Are they few enough to assure your ability to deal with the essence of your job, yet not so few that they make planning difficult?
- Do they overlap someone else's responsibility? Or "under-lap," leaving no one responsible for the desired result?
- Do they align vertically so that your results mesh well with those above and below you?
- Do they align horizontally so that your results mesh well with those on the same level?

[ARE YOU AN EFFECTIVE LEADER?]

"The greatest risk is to risk nothing."

Long ago, Peter Drucker introduced us to the concept that leaders can be identified by these qualities:

- Leaders start projects by asking, "What has to be done?" instead of "What do I need?"
- Leaders continually ask, "What are my organization's purposes and objectives?" and "What qualifies as acceptable performance and adds to the bottom line?"

- Leaders don't want clones of themselves. They never ask, "Do I like or dislike this person?" but they won't tolerate poor performance.

- Leaders aren't threatened by others who have strengths they lack.

Drucker's conclusions are directly applicable to a practical current definition of competitiveness. Try it. Substitute the word "competitors" for "leaders" in each of the above statements and you will see what I mean.

[CARING CANNOT BE FAKED]

No matter how you slice it, caring can't be faked. But being truly caring is a critical component to having a positive toward those around you. Cynics suggest that people don't care as much as they once did. Others say that people care too much, especially about themselves.

To complicate the matter, even social scientists admit there are a lot of unanswered questions. For instance, how do we learn how to care? When do we show it? Who are the caregivers? Does it apply to business? Can caring be taught?

Jack Beasley, Professor of Family and Child Studies at Georgia Southern College, says the ability to care is also associated with one's willingness or desire to see another person's point of view or needs, and act accordingly. Beasley, also a corporate consultant on family issues, believes that caring is a skill and learning how to care is a lifelong process. Even if you didn't experience caring in childhood, you can learn how to care in adulthood. In fact, many of the techniques associated with child caring maximize productivity and improve relationships.

If you want to improve your ability to care, Professor Beasley offers these techniques to begin:

1. Study individuals in situations where their team is losing.

2. Demonstrate caring. Employees who see their supervisors and colleagues as caring about them are more productive.

3. Do not smother. Part of caring is to know when to hold back. Give what is appropriate to the care and need of the individual, but don't overkill. *Don't do for others what they can do for themselves.* If you do too much, individuals will devalue both you and their own abilities.

4. Care enough to allow people to learn from logical consequence. You can tell people what will happen, but they usually have to experience it themselves to be believers.

5. Keep your own needs in check. Care is a by-product of self-esteem. Individuals who are content with themselves and their abilities don't have as much to prove as those struggling to determine who they are and what they stand for. One way to foster the development of others and keep your own needs in check is to encourage them to enhance their own abilities. Then they can take all the credit.

6. Finally, care for yourself. Caring for your self is not selfish. *You can't show you care for others if you don't care for yourself.*

There is a boomerang effect of faking caring. Mark Twain's advice is solid: "If you tell the truth, you don't have to remember anything."

When you truly don't care about people, they will see through you and the results will be demotivated, unhappy people. On the other hand, when you do truly care, those around you will notice and respond. You will find that you naturally:

- Challenge people with meaningful work assignments.
- Complement them on jobs well done.
- Stand behind decisions affecting their welfare.
- Pay careful attention to *their* needs versus what you *think* their needs are.

If you are a manager or you aspire to be, you are obliged, for your own sake, to think carefully about your motives for wanting to be in management. Ask yourself whether you can truly be interested in the welfare of your people. If your honest answer is "No" or even, "I'm not sure," it will do little good to pretend. Plainly and simply, caring can't be faked. If you doubt that, ask yourself, "Of the fakes I know, who would I follow?"

CHAPTER 4

MOTIVATING OTHERS

*"First say to yourself what you would be;
and then do what you have to do"*
—Epicetus

If you are a manager or supervisor, how your attitude influences and motivates others will be apparent in their behavior. If you are not yet a manager, you can still be a leader, and your attitude will affect those around you as well. To ultimately grow into a management role, you want to be noticed as someone who brings out the best in those around them. People who are not motivated to do their best frequently don't because they honestly feel that you don't really care about them.

As a supervisor, your job is to meld your team members into a cohesive group and work with them to develop within themselves the inner motivation to accomplish the team's goals. This process starts by taking the time to know your colleagues as individuals. Each has strengths and weaknesses. Understanding each individual is the first step in building a motivated *group* of people.

This requires more than just knowing job skills. It means learning what's important to each person in terms of ambitions, goals, families, and special concerns away from work.

You must show you appreciate good work and you must treat team members with respect. When people meet expectations, don't hesitate to praise them. When there are problems, step in to help by helping people figure out ways to overcome obstacles. This way they will rely on you and know they can turn to you when they are struggling.

[DEALING WITH OVERACHIEVERS]

The benefits from a positive attitude come more from how you handle overachievers rather than underachievers. Why? Because they are the ones who provide the cutting edge for your organization's future. Most managers spend too much time working to improve the performance of underachievers. This is important, but not if overachievers are neglected. These highly competent people offer the kind of opportunity every manager should welcome. But unless carefully coached, high-potential people can create problems for themselves as well as for the organization. Because go-getters are frequently nonconformists and, because they are not afraid to speak their minds, some managers find them irritating and presumptuous, even intimidating.

Here are some powerful ways to harness the energy of those who want to move ahead rapidly:

- Delegate. Provide opportunities for increasing skills by doing things under pressure and, of course, under careful supervision. Provide assignments that not only challenge their capabilities and drive, but that offer the training essential for future promotions as well.

- Use the incentive of recognition. There's real power in recognition by publicly praising and rewarding outstanding performance. The opposite is also very important. Never criticize publicly; always in private.

- Offer promotions on a temporary basis to test abilities and see how they respond to new situations.

Employees who don't really care, who have no deep-seated feelings of loyalty to an employer are rarely, if ever, among the overachievers. Carefully handled, these men and women have great value. They do not hesitate to suggest, recommend, advise, and change things, which conformists are seldom able or likely to do. Every organization needs these overachievers.

[COMMUNICATING EFFECTIVELY]

Communication is as much attitude as it is technique. Where conversation is involved, for example, it must have purpose. It should always be constructive. You should always recognize that problems and questions raised by others are important to you.

To secure better cooperation from your colleagues, try these tips:

1. Share information while it's still fresh. In other words, let people know what they need to know as much in advance as possible.

2. When you are discussing something, focus on how it is important to whomever you are speaking to rather than on what it means to you.

3. Be generous in sharing viewpoints. Ask, "Are you comfortable with that? What's your reaction to . . . ? What if I said . . .?"

4. When in doubt, don't hesitate to call in an expert. Remember, you are not paid to know everything about everything yourself.

5. Most people who feel they are experienced in a particular field are likely to talk too much. Try to use as few words as possible. Excess words usually create confusion, boredom, and loss of interest.

[BECOMING A BETTER LISTENER]

Usually we think of communication as speaking or writing. They are both essential, but not the only aspects of overall communication. Listening, not just passively, but active, participative listening is vital. And being a good listener sends strong, positive feedback to those around you, as it tells them you think they are important and worth your time. Much of your effectiveness rests on the skills with which you understand others, the attitude you have when listening, and the level of involvement you demonstrate.

These four time-tested steps will improve listening skills. You must:

1. Listen to clarify.
2. Listen to check the meaning and interpretation of others.
3. Listen to show understanding.
4. Listen to get feedback.

Listening is hard work. It's more than just keeping your ears open. Let's say a colleague brings a problem to you and asks for help. At first you listen attentively. But it's not long before your mind begins to wander. Instead of listening to the problem, you're thinking about other things: the pile of work on your desk, the meeting you have scheduled with the company vice president, or the problems one of your children is having at school. You *hear* the words, but you're not really *listening*.

This happens because the human mind can process ideas many times faster than anyone can talk. While someone is talking, your mind may race ahead. You complete the speaker's sentence in your mind—often incorrectly—long before their words come out. You "hear" what your mind dictates, not what's actually said.

This is human nature. The solution is to anticipate it will happen, and take steps to overcome the tendency. It's embarrassing to admit you weren't listening, so you fake it. You pick up on the last few words and comment on them. Sometimes you get back on track, but often may miss the real message.

If you haven't been listening, you can recover by asking, "Can we go back to what you said?" or "Would you mind repeating that, I'm not sure I understand."

Good listeners are actively involved and tend to follow these guidelines:

- Look at the speaker. Eye contact is the first way of showing interest, but don't overdo it. Look at the whole person; don't just stare at their eyes.

- Let your facial expressions indicate you are connecting.

- Demonstrate you are following the conversation by nods or gestures.

- Ask specific questions about specific points. This not only enables you to clarify what may be unclear but also keeps you alert and paying full attention.

- Don't interrupt. A pause should not be a signal for you to start talking. Wait. The other person may have more to say.

- Be an empathic listener. Listen with your heart as well as your head. In other words, try to put yourself in the speaker's shoes.

You can become a better listener. Everyone around you will respond to your positive attention to them and what they have to say. A small effort can gain a big return!

[ASK THE RIGHT QUESTIONS]

Questioning is as important as listening. The power of a good question lies in the fact that it compels a pertinent answer. If we ask the right questions, we will get better answers, in terms of information, experience, and reactions. Asking the right questions tells others that you value them and are listening and caring about what they have to say. Wrong questions beg for wrong answers.

Asking is more essential to progress than telling. Why? Because we all need adequate information to be effective. Indeed, decisions are only as good as the information on which we base them.

[MAKING CRITICISM CONSTRUCTIVE]

"Ninety-nine percent of failures come from people who have the habit of making excuses."
—GEORGE WASHINGTON CARVER

Before criticizing, probe to be certain you know the performance problem. Then make constructive suggestions about how to improve. It can be very difficult to maintain a positive attitude when you need to point out a problem. If people around you get the impression that you are always complaining, your effectiveness will plummet. The key to effectively criticizing others is, in fact, to keep it positive. Focus on solutions and improvements. Encourage others in their ability to take positive action and effect change. Instead of being labeled a complainer you will be looked at as a source of innovative thinking and positive change.

[TEAMING]

"The essence of a team is common commitment. Without it,
the members of a group perform as individuals; with it
they become a powerful unit for collective performance."
—ARTHUR R. PELL

Being part of a team always brings new challenges. The way you feel about your team members will be reflected in your attitude as well as in the environment you help establish.

Creative thinking should always be encouraged. It can yield not only practical ideas but also gain the commitment needed to make an idea or suggestion work on the job.

Winning teams are built when people are directly involved in day-to-day decisions, can see the results achieved, and are recognized for outstanding performance.

How would you rate as a team leader? What qualities do you believe are important? Information obtained from a study of over 5,000 employees showed some insights into how people viewed their bosses. The participants worked for more than a dozen businesses and government agencies. This information highlighted ten essential qualities or characteristics viewed as a requirement for a successful team leader. The same qualities were identified, whether the manager was a man or a woman, regardless of age, size or location of the industry, organizational structure, or corporate culture. The following quiz focuses on these ten qualities. After each item, rate yourself in one of three categories: as "S" for Strong, "A" for Average, or "W" for Weak. Then ask five other people who know you well to rate you on the same items.

1._____ Providing clear directions

2._____ Encouraging open, two-way communication

3._____ Willingness to coach and support people

4._____ Providing objective recognition

5._____ Establishing ongoing controls

6._____ Selecting the right people to staff the organization

7._____ Understanding the financial implications of decisions

8._____ Encouraging innovation and new ideas

9._____ Giving clear-cut decisions when they are needed

10._____ Consistently demonstrating high levels of integrity

Compare how you rated yourself with responses of the others. Discuss areas of difference. Find out why. Give examples. Arrange the weaknesses in priority, so you can systematically work to correct them.

How you view yourself sometimes contrasts starkly with others. You might see yourself as diplomatic, while they see you as patronizing. What you feel is a cautious move others may see as indecisiveness. You may not be aware that you are viewed as abrasive and difficult to be around. You may not realize your effect on others until you get a pinpointed analysis of your behavior.

[DEVELOPING YOUR INTERPERSONAL RELATIONSHIPS]

Of course a key ingredient to positively affecting those around you is to have positive relationships with others. The following ten questions will help you look at yourself more objectively so you can determine if you are a positive influence in the office. To each one, answer yes or no. Be honest. Don't defend the behavior. Even though we know the circumstances and motivations behind our behaviors, others only see the action.

---

1. Are you condescendingly critical? When talking of others in the organization, do you speak of straightening them out?

Yes _____ No _____

2. Do you need to be in full control? Does almost everything need to be cleared with you?

Yes _____ No _____

3. In meetings, do your comments take a disproportionate amount of time?

Yes _____ No _____

4. Are you quick to attack?

Yes _____ No _____

5. Are you reluctant to let others have the same privileges or perquisites as you?

Yes _____ No _____

6. When talking, do you use the word "I" often?

Yes _____ No _____

7. Do others admire you because you are strong and capable, or because of your position and status?

Yes _____ No _____

(continues)

8. Do people speak of you as cold and distant, but you really want them to like you?

Yes _____ No _____

9. Do you regard yourself as more competent than your peers? Your boss? Does your behavior show it?

Yes _____ No _____

10. Do you enjoy acquiring symbols of status and power?

Yes _____ No _____

If you answered yes to three to five of these questions, your behavior is probably perceived as abrasive. If you answered yes to six or more, you may have a serious problem.

How others perceive you has a direct effect on their morale. If this seems to be a problem, one of the first places to look is your attitude. You may need to make changes. More and more companies are retaining the services of executive coaches to help managers see themselves as others see them and guide them to improvement.

[IMPROVING MORALE]

Morale cannot be bestowed. If those around you are assertive, express their career goals cordially, and feel their training needs are attended to, good morale has a chance. It rises when a partnership develops between managers and employees. When you can, empower others and it will enhance morale.

When they believe they can initiate action, exert some control over their work, and are involved in decision making, morale will be enhanced.

[CHANGE BEFORE YOU MUST]

Change is often viewed as scary. But a positive attitude can help you see change in a better light. While it doesn't come easily, it can be less troublesome if you:

1. Think objectively. Where are you now? How did you get there? Where will you be in the future if you don't do anything differently?

2. Scan wider horizons. What changes would eliminate the threats or dangers you face?

3. Increase your visibility. To stand out from others, your goals must be higher than theirs.

4. Keep your options open. Use your best talents to create more options.

People who plan and prepare outperform those who don't. To avoid unwanted surprises:

*   Become an expert at what you do.

*   Know what resources you need, as well as where and how to get them.

*   Shift those resources to get the highest yield.

*   Set up an *objective* system to measure progress.

*   Take a realistic view of the future—don't trust opinions that aren't based on fact.

*   Budget time carefully.

*   Become the best example of self-discipline.

*   Stay away from negative people.

[LEVERAGE YOUR ABILITIES]

"More failure results from indecision than wrong choices."

Almost everyone has felt a need to change directions. Maybe they believe they have reached their limit where they are. Maybe a new opportunity has opened up. Maybe they are tired of doing the same thing day after day. Whatever the motivation, when that happens, consider these three keys to focus on your strengths when you are in a period of transition:

- *Expect obstacles.* Ask for criticism and feedback. If your convictions are strong enough, you will find ways to overcome any obstacles that may stand in your way.

- *Don't expect miracles.* When you start from a fresh new beginning, realize that progress will take time. Stay focused on your eventual goal.

- *Refuse to settle for less than your best.* Seek responsibility. Success will come when you find a role that allows you to creatively use a combination of your abilities. Don't avoid what you do best. Find a balance between your talents and your interests.

Charles Kettering, founder of Delco and former Vice President of General Motors, was a self-made inventor-mogul, topped only by Thomas Edison. Kettering, who held over 200 patents, was known for the electronic self-starter found in most car engines today. He was also a pioneer in the development of diesel engines, anti-knock gas, home air conditioning units, and quick-drying paint for cars.

He had little time for traditional schooling and contended that, "Overly educated people were the ones least likely to make new discoveries because they were too intent on doing things the way they had been taught."

Eyestrain was a problem for Kettering, so classmates read aloud to him, teaching him to rely on his own inner vision, giving him a better mental picture to draw from. His positive attitude enabled him to use his abilities to the fullest in spite of his eye problems. Some would maintain that he achieved so much "because of" his eye problems.

[AVOID DOUBTERS]

"Optimists see possibilities. Pessimists refuse to look."

If the people who influence you most are always concerned about what can't be done, you are liable to join them. Doubters and pessimists stay the same or get worse. Avoid these "mildewed" people (afflicted by a fungus from being in the dark too long), if you believe things can be better.

In 1920, Robert Goddard, a physics professor at Clark University in Worcester, Massachusetts, wrote a paper expressing the belief that man could build a rocket capable of reaching the moon. The story appeared in newspapers throughout the world. Some of them weren't very kind. *The New York Times* and the *London Graphic*, for example, said that it was impossible for a rocket to perform in space because it would not have gravity to push against. Another paper rudely stated that Goddard lacked "the knowledge ladled out daily in high schools." He was not discouraged. "Every vision is a joke," he announced, "until the first man accomplishes it."

To be successful in space, he knew a rocket would require a new fuel to propel it. He began to work on mixtures of liquid hydrogen and liquid oxygen. The hydrogen would propel the rocket; the oxygen would replace the air needed to keep the fuel burning.

In 1926, Goddard built and launched a 10-foot rocket that

reached a speed of 60 mph, stayed in the air 2.5 seconds, and climbed to an altitude of 41 feet. He was encouraged, but knew that a rocket would have to reach the speed of at least 25,000 mph in order to escape Earth's gravity. He built models near Roswell, New Mexico, where he sent 14-, 16-, and 18-foot rockets to altitudes of 2,000, 7,500, and 9,000 feet. One exceeded the speed of sound. Another featured revolutionary fin-stabilized steering.

When World War II came along, Goddard's technology produced rockets for use by airplanes. Before his death in 1945, he had 214 patents and was acknowledged as a pioneer in modern rocketry. He was and continues to be recognized as the father of space flight. He overcame all doubters.

[LEAN FORWARD AND DON'T LOOK BACK]

War provides few opportunities for error. Military commanders who second-guess themselves usually lose. Decisions must be made instantaneously and the stakes are very, very high. Examples set by some of history's greatest military leaders carry valuable lessons for everyone who wants to improve.

Ulysses S. Grant. Of him, President Abraham Lincoln once said: "I cannot spare this man. He fights." Told that Grant also liked to drink, Lincoln replied: "Tell me his brand so that I may send the same to all my generals." Gen. William T. Sherman added: "I know more about strategy, logistics, and every aspect of military employment than he (Grant). However, there is one aspect in which Grant beats me and everyone else. He runs into problems and they don't bother him. He keeps pressing on."

Hannibal. The Romans knew about Hannibal's plan to lead a herd of elephants through the Alps and into Rome, but they said it couldn't be done. Hannibal responded: "We will find a way or make one." And he did.

Adm. David Farragut. At the battle of Mobile Bay in August 1864, Farragut commanded a fleet of four ironclad monitors and 14 wooden ships. As he sailed into the Confederate gunfire, a mine destroyed his leading monitor. The fleet stopped cold. Some of Farragut's officers urged him to retreat; instead, he had himself strapped to the rigging of his flagship, the *USS Hartford*, ordered his ship into the minefield, and issued the famous command: "Damn the torpedoes! Full speed ahead!"

"Courageous people look fear in the face and say, "Bring it on!"

Napoleon Bonaparte. Asked about his talent for planning and thinking ahead, Napoleon replied: "If I always appear prepared, it is because, before entering an undertaking, I have thought a long time and tried to foresee what may occur. It is not genius which reveals to me suddenly and secretly what I should do in circumstances unexpected by others. It is meditation and preparation."

"You lead not by what you say, but by what you do."

CHAPTER 5

MAXIMIZING YOUR PERFORMANCE

"For success, attitude is equally as important as ability."
—HARRY F. BANKS

Attitude determines behavior. The first question addressing this issue is, are you accountable?

[ACCEPT RESPONSIBILITY FOR YOUR ACTIONS]

Peter Drucker wisely points out that effective executives must develop character, foresight, self-reliance, and courage. Organizations, he reminds us, are made up of ordinary people who together must do extraordinary things. This cannot happen if people avoid responsibility.

People must be taught to be accountable.

Assuming responsibility may be hard, but if you don't take charge, fearing that you may do something wrong, then you have failed. Long-term success requires the willingness to take charge when needed and risk failure.

No one is blessed with infallible judgment. The person hasn't been born who always makes the right move.

This point is illustrated by the woman who was promoted to a major marketing position. Upon completing her first assignment on the new job, she was shocked to find she had made a serious error, which resulted in the failure of the project and a cost to the company of over $100,000. When her boss called her into his office, she apologized and said, "I guess you are going to fire me now." The boss responded, "Fire you? No way, I just spent $100,000 training you."

[THINK BEFORE YOU DECIDE]

You can sharpen and improve your judgment by disciplining yourself to consider fundamentals:

- Take time to think things through. Whenever you're faced with a problem, control the impulse to rush headlong into action. Reason things out first. Try to foresee how things might turn out.

- For each possible solution, list the possible good and bad, the costs, the risks, problems, and objections that could arise.

- Be objective. Look at the facts. Those who don't want to be bothered by the facts because they've already made up their minds are asking for trouble.

- Keep your preconceptions, prejudices, and personal dislikes out of it. Try to visualize the reactions of other people. Your intended action may make a lot of sense to you but what about associates? If you were in their shoes, what would you think was the wisest thing to do? The best-laid plans are likely to fail if the people involved won't cooperate. Take a good look down every road that's open before you choose the one to follow.

• Face the fact that criticism is inevitable.

[EXPECT PROBLEMS]

A common failing of many managers is to ignore a problem rather than face it and take responsibility for deciding one way or another.

After all, people who don't make decisions can't be criticized for poor judgment. The president of a leading corporation known for his ability in developing associates dismisses most errors of judgment with a stock comment: "All right, that's behind us, now what's our next move?"

He encourages people to make decisions, encourages managers to manage. What he wants is action and a winning average, a company that moves instead of resting on its laurels for fear of making mistakes. The record shows in this case that he usually gets what he wants. Remember, life is a batting average. It's never perfect.

"What happens to us is less important
than what we make happen."

[PERCEPTION CAN BE REALITY]

No matter how high or low on the managerial ladder, you should know that *how* you say something is at least as important as *what* you say. Your attitude toward employees and coworkers will ring out loud and clear. You may think: "Is this just busywork?" "Is my boss just dumping this on me because she doesn't want to deal with it?" "Is this just a useless exercise in information gathering that will never see the light of day? Will my work really have an impact somewhere?" How do your people perceive your orders, directions, and ideas?

When you ask associates to do something, be sure to also tell them why. It's well worth the time and effort. It's very easy for a busy person to fall into the habit of simply telling without explanation. It seems like the quickest and easiest way to get things done. But it's rarely the best way. When you ask someone to do something, take the time to explain why. It's an excellent habit with many benefits.

Explaining why you want something done automatically removes the curse of bossiness. When there's a good reason why something ought to be done it puts you in the position of simply making a logical, reasonable request. It completely removes the bad taste that comes from direct orders.

When you explain why, you also lessen the chance of errors. People who understand why they're doing things are less apt to make mistakes. And if the situations change so that the actions are no longer required, they'll have sense enough to stop and bring it to your attention.

If they don't understand, they will tend to go blindly ahead doing what you told them to do. It's an excellent copout. Things go wrong, a person can always fall back on the notion, "That's what they told me to do; I was only carrying out orders." Even worse, they may have perceived your direction differently from what you had in mind and been chugging away in the wrong direction.

Explaining the reasons for your requests are a compliment to the people you've asked to carry them out. It shows what you think is important, provides needed background information, and encourages them to use their own heads.

You also put them in the position to make suggestions, which can often be very helpful. People aren't robots. You don't get them to think by pushing their button. The more you treat them like intelligent human beings with good brains in their heads, the better your results will be.

Sure, there are times when a reason is so obvious to everyone it isn't worth mentioning. And there are also times of emergency, when people have to do what they're told and pronto. But the general rule still stands. When you ask someone to do something, explain why.

[KNOW YOUR COLLEAGUES]

A close examination of people who have achieved success in business usually reveals that four factors are almost always present. They have:

1. An inclination to think before taking action

2. An inner drive

3. A willingness to assume responsibility

4. The ability to lead people

This means learning to recognize talent and accomplishment, even as people change. Some grow and develop; others slip into complacency and apathy.

A good leader keeps abreast of these changes whether for good or bad. Long-time employees who have done their jobs for so long it's hard to picture them doing anything else are often taken for granted. They don't complain so you tend not to think about them.

The truth may be, however, they've outgrown the job and are ready for something bigger. Many people, locked in their companies, have quietly accepted other jobs and surprised former associates by moving rapidly ahead to greater achievement. Why? Because the new employers took a fresh look at their capabilities and gave them a chance to use them.

To keep good people from becoming frustrated, it's necessary to notice their developing talents. Find a way to put them to use. "The only person who behaves sensibly," said George Bernard Shaw, "is my tailor. He takes my measure anew every time he sees me. All the rest go on with their old measurements."

True, some people reach the limits of their ability. Greater demands would only get them in over their heads. But most people keep learning and growing, far more than their bosses recognize. Keeping people in jobs they've outgrown isn't good for them or for the company.

Realistically speaking, required work gets priority. Still, you can usually find ways to give people more challenges. If they are doing well in their present assignments, what else can they do? Is there some way to test their capacity with other tasks? If they've mastered one responsibility can you enlarge it by assigning something new? When they show special abilities, give them more complex problems in that area. It keeps them reaching and growing.

Whatever you do, try not to underrate people. A new look may surprise you. Visualize the man or woman in a more challenging situation. What counts is not what they were capable of yesterday but what they can do today and tomorrow.

When management at GM recognized that the company's market share was shrinking at a time when other U.S. carmakers were generally making up ground against the Japanese, they brought in a man named H. Ross Perot by purchasing a company he had created and developed to be a leader in its field. He was a maverick, but very successful.

Unfortunately, GM's leaders refused to listen to the outsider. Even as Perot was evaluating the bloated, paralytic carmaker, top management was trying to figure out how to remove him. He was a thorn in their side. It was a clash between new ideas and an inbred commitment to repetition and resistance to change. As is often the case, repetition won.

"Encourage your associates to express their ideas, especially when they differ from yours. Their disagreements not only provide you with new ideas, but give you insight into the way they approach problems that will help you work more effectively with them."
—FRANKLIN C. ASHBY

[POSITIVE ATTITUDE ENCOURAGES IMPROVED PERFORMANCE]

Not only does attitude affect morale, self-esteem, and behavior, it directly impacts the bottom line. Your job as a manager is to help employees reach optimum productivity. These suggestions are basic:

1. Pass on information to upper management about suggestions or progressive ideas of coworkers and team members.

2. Encourage people to think creatively and provide an environment in which they are not laughed at or criticized when they do.

3. Never take credit for ideas generated by others. When you acknowledge the person with the idea rather than taking credit yourself, they will tend to have even better ones.

4. Provide people with work they feel is important. There's no greater lift than the successful completion of a job that contributes measurably to improvement.

5. Let people know that they belong. Help them understand what is special about being associated with your firm.

6. Stimulate thinking about the importance of what your work group does. All too often, people are not impressed by their work because they are led to believe no one else cares or thinks "anyone could do it."

7. Remember, while employees work for money, most also want participation, recognition, belonging, and achievement. When these benefits are present, an obsession with money alone is less likely to mount, if reasonable standards of compensation fairness are met.

"Ability is what you're capable of doing. Motivation determines what you do. Attitude determines how well you do it."
—LOU HOLTZ

[THE GENERATION GAP]

Much is being written these days about a generation gap in attitudes toward work. This would include acceptance of authority and the place of experience in getting promoted.

Professor Quinn Mills of Harvard University has done extensive research on characteristics related to productivity. He found that age differences do, in fact, stand out strongly but there are no differences in values by ethnic background and no differences between people in different types of jobs or different sectors of the economy. Reporting on a series of surveys and interviews with more than a thousand managers, and more than one thousand employees at companies nationwide, the Harvard study found these generation gaps.

- The older generation, products of the World War II era, accepts authority. Members of the younger generation, generally called the "baby boomers," having grown up during the Vietnam era, typically do not trust authority.

- The older generation sees work as a duty, an instrument through which they can support themselves and their families. The younger generation believes work should be fun, enjoyable, and more social. Work has become the major place to meet for younger people, along with health clubs, etc.

- The older generation believes experience is the necessary road to promotion, and is willing to spend time in apprenticeship with the expectation of a reward for spending that time. The younger generation sees no reason to wait, believing that people should advance just as quickly as their performance permits.

- The older generation believes in tact. The younger generation demands honesty and candor. To them, tact is seen as evasion of the issues.

- The older generation believes that fairness is achieved by treating everyone the same. The younger generation believes that fairness requires that individuals should be allowed to be different.

- The older generation gives attention to possessions and status. The younger generation gives attention to experiences.

Since this research began, the WWII generation has moved into retirement and the baby boomer generation is now the predominant age in management positions. Their children and grandchildren, often called Gen-X and Gen-Y, have a still different outlook on life. They tend to be independent thinkers and are often resistant to authority. As they enter the workforce in the early years of the twenty-first century, managers will have to learn more about their expectations and attitudes to effectively deal with them.

These differences become increasingly significant as the proportion of younger people decreases. As this happens, serious labor shortages develop and we must pay more attention to generation gaps.

There are some benefits of inexperience, believe it or not. If you are skeptical about hiring young people who have no background in your business, think about the advantages of the way Patrick Kelly and Bill Riddell of Physician Sales and Services, Inc., go about it. They believe that some routine jobs can be done much more enthusiastically by inexperienced people, if and when they know there's a plan for their advancement.

"We sell them on the idea that what they're doing now is temporary," says Riddell. "Six months not two years is a reasonable time for them to expect something new to do." As a result they get highly motivated young men and women to drive delivery vans and sweep the floors.

They also believe it is essential to show people how to do things "their way." Most, they find, who have worked for other companies have attitudes they must put aside. In other words, they have to "unlearn" a lot of things before they can move ahead.

Riddell has discovered that, "By hiring inexperienced people you can spread your culture better and faster." In the instances where they do hire people with a lot of experience or an extensive background in their industry, they literally surround them with others who haven't had much experience. That way they can begin to turn a work group in the direction they want it to go much faster.

Another good example is Enterprise Rent-a-Car, which hires over 7,000 management trainees a year recruited from 220 campuses all over the world. These trainees start at the very bottom, washing cars and picking up customers. Those who succeed do these menial jobs willingly and enthusiastically because they know there is opportunity to move rapidly up the corporate ladder.

> *"He who would accomplish little must sacrifice little.*
> *He who would accomplish much must sacrifice much."*
> —JAMES ALLEN

CHAPTER 6

SHARPENING YOUR INTERPERSONAL SKILLS

*"A positive attitude quickly sorts out the
options that yield best results."*

The greatest problems in the workplace aren't due to technical competence but to lack of people skills. How you relate to coworkers makes the difference between success and failure. Most situations are not complicated, and can be improved by some very simple actions.

- *Show consideration of others.* Consideration for other people is shown by arriving on time, taking only allotted time for meals and other breaks, limiting personal phone calls and e-mails, leaving personal problems at home, respecting the property of others, not wasting time, dressing in accordance with reasonably prescribed standards, respecting confidentiality, and avoiding destructive gossip.

- *Communicate areas of concern before they become major issues.* Don't let something fester to the point where it's beyond the crisis stage and very little can be done.

- *Take the initiative.* Respect the chain of command when it is expected, but provide assistance to others when possible.

"Pretend that every single person you meet has a sign around his or her neck that says MAKE ME FEEL IMPORTANT. *Not only will you succeed in sales, you will succeed in life."*
—MARY KAYE ASH

[PREPARING FOR CHANGE]

Progress almost always requires change. Your attitude determines in large part how you prepare for and adjust to it.

Change isn't comfortable. It makes us uncertain and uneasy. Even when a change seems reasonable and logical, we still ask ourselves: "Who knows how this will work out? Why not leave things as they are?"

We seem to be instinctively opposed to new ideas that might alter our lives, yet realize that those who don't experiment find themselves falling behind. These strategies can help:

- Try to see that new ideas get a fair test. Don't introduce them as something drastically new and radical, which you intend to put into effect right away. Discuss them casually as options.

- Emphasize the points of similarity with things you've already done successfully or others have done. Let people think about it for a while. Then bring it up again.

- Mention additional advantages that have occurred to you but don't push too hard. Talk about it as an interesting possibility. Listen to other opinions. A few small changes made sequentially over a period of time might be much less upsetting than one big one.

- If resistance is obviously too great, it may be wise to drop it for a while. But don't forget it. Bring it up later in a form that might raise fewer objections, or when timing is more favorable. Remember, logic alone will not win your case. You may be able to force change on some people but you can't make them like it. Do your best to get some buy-in before you force the issue.

Change is essential to progress but rarely easy to accomplish. Acknowledging this in advance is a key factor in gauging the degree of difficulty. A positive attitude toward change will help you—and everyone around you—accept it more easily.

[OVERCOMING RESISTANCE TO CHANGE]

Resistance to change at work shows in many ways, including increases in absenteeism, employee turnover, requests for transfer, complaints, less cooperation, reluctance to give full support when a new system is introduced, and reduced productivity.

The most obvious resistance relates to changes that may result in the loss of job, decrease in the value of skills, or reduction in pay.

The two most reliable ways to gain continuing support for new ideas are to: (1) encourage participation and (2) prevent resentment.

Encourage Participation

What lingering problems do you face? Can you isolate the reasons? Have you started to work on them? Whether you are attempting to solve a serious problem or doing routine work, receiving suggestions will be a key to your ultimate success.

Successful leaders understand and acknowledge that most people like to make suggestions. When they don't, it's usually because their managers have made it clear one way or another that they really aren't interested in what they have to say. Result? They aren't going to waste much time trying to think of new and better ways. No matter how brilliant you may be, it's a mistake to ignore the brains and ideas of the people involved with you.

The people who actually handle a job day after day are in the best position to figure out how it might be done better. With a little encouragement, they will usually come up with some excellent ideas.

Leaders are judged not merely by their own performance, but by the total efforts of their team. Managers who fail to establish a climate in which associates are encouraged to think and present new ideas will never know what their potential might be.

Have you noticed the best managers usually have the most able assistants? That's more than coincidence. It's because they deliberately set out to develop them. They encourage people to think and take responsibility for improving their own performance.

The best way to get more suggestions is to simply ask for them. Whenever you have a problem, talk it over with the people involved and let them all contribute. Most are pleased to be consulted.

Show your appreciation for all suggestions. Take time to think about all you get. Give satisfaction by taking a tactful amount of time before answering.

Rejecting Suggestions Without Causing Resentment

Margo Marston called her staff together to discuss a problem. Diane, a new associate, proposed a solution. Margo's immediate response: "We tried that before and it didn't work." Now it was true that they did try something like that before unsuccessfully, but Diane interprets this as "She doesn't want my ideas." Not only was she resentful, she felt there was no point in presenting ideas if they are automatically rejected.

How could Margo have rejected the idea without causing Diane's negative reaction?

1. *Do it privately.* Never reject suggestions in front of others. Thank Diane for the suggestion and say that you will get back to her. As soon as possible, meet and go over the idea. After she repeats her suggestion, say, "We tried something like that two years ago and we had serious problems with it." Note the difference in the choice of words. "It didn't work" is final. There's no way this can be salvaged. The second approach, "We had problems with it," keeps the door open. Diane might then ask "What were the problems?" Once she learns, she may respond, "I didn't think about that. I should give it more thought." Or perhaps she may say, "I considered that possibility and have some ideas on how we can avoid it."

2. *Ask the right questions.* Socrates never told one of his students that he was wrong. If a student came up with an incorrect answer, Socrates asked another question. By carefully wording the questions, he encouraged his pupils to think out the problem and come up with the right solution. Follow the lead of this great teacher. By carefully questioning Diane, Margo could have enabled her to rethink, reevaluate, and prepare a more viable idea. With good questioning, Diane could have reconsidered her original idea and replaced it with a better one.

When you turn down suggestions, do it gently. Let there be no doubt you appreciate the ideas and want more. The next one may be terrific.

> *"Give thanks and celebrate a positive attitude.*
> *It enables you to test your potential every day."*

CHAPTER 7

OVERCOMING PROBLEMS TOGETHER

"Do what you can, with what you have, where you are."
—THEODORE ROOSEVELT

[WHEN THINGS GO WRONG]

Circumstances change. Mistakes are inevitable. The best policy when things go wrong is to pause and examine. Maintain a positive attitude: don't be in a hurry to accuse anybody of anything. First, find out what really happened. Ask questions calmly, slowly, and methodically.

Getting excited and emotional only makes matters worse. Punishment is the worst motivator because it may cause people to duck responsibility for anything that might go wrong in the future.

The goal is not to make people feel guilty or incompetent. It is to prompt them to do better in the future by ensuring they know how. In other words, be a friendly troubleshooter. Help employees look for what's wrong. Be sure they understand the reasons for doing a better job.

Resist the temptation to criticize hastily. When people do poor work, ask questions and find the reasons. *Then attack the reasons, not the person.*

Frequently we must work with people who aren't like us or maybe even don't like us. The aim is to work together productively and find ways to avoid conflict. These suggestions will help:

- *Pay a compliment.* For example, you might say, "Good idea. Could you expand on that and make it a little clearer for me?" The hostile person often lacks self-esteem yet needs to feel important.

- *Resist the temptation to argue.* Confrontation encourages hostile people to be more intense. Taking that lure away from them will be disarming. Seek areas of agreement even if they are difficult to find.

The worst reaction to hostility is humiliation; when you humiliate someone you have made an enemy, count on it.

[DEALING WITH CONFLICT]

Hostility is not the only unavoidable encounter in life. Opposition and conflict are also inevitable. Neither is terrible by definition. The controlling factor is attitude. Do we reflect an outlook that views conflict and opposition as situations to be avoided at all costs or do we believe that conflict can sometimes be positive and opposition helpful?

Effective people utilize ways to minimize the negative consequences of conflict. Here are some dependable guidelines.

1. Face-to-face meetings between opponents are essential. This is the only way to be certain you know their position.

2. Don't hide your views. In the first meeting, bring them out into the open. If you can handle the relationship first you are on the road to an agreement.

3. Minimize status differences. When confronting a conflict head-on, it is best to keep the opposing parties on reasonable equal footing.

4. Don't try to place blame. In a problem-solving approach, placing blame serves no useful purpose.

5. Deal with conflict at the lowest possible level. Too often, managers get themselves involved in conflicts that should be handled by employees themselves. Clearly there are times you must get involved, but if you do it too often, you will become a referee and waste much valuable time in the process.

6. Delay commitments to specific solutions. Too much time can make matters worse, but some interval may help all participants hold open their options and be more flexible about an ultimate best solution.

7. Identify areas of mutual agreement. To achieve this, list early the items on which all parties can agree.

8. Emphasize mutual benefits. This will highlight concrete reasons to cooperate.

9. Use language that does not evaluate, that is not judgmental. Sometimes our language reveals feelings without our being aware of it.

10. When errors cause a conflict, be specific. Avoid generalities and sweeping statements like, "You *always* seem to disagree" or "You're *never* very helpful."

11. Build coalitions for handling future conflicts. By building on success from the past you will be in a better position to deal with the ones still to come.

12. Examine your own biases and feelings first. Keep them from interfering with your desires for a satisfactory resolution.

[GIVING CRITICISM]

Acceptance of criticism can be increased significantly using these methods:

- Begin with a positive approach by asking for an assessment of the successes achieved and the steps taken to achieve them.
- Then talk about projects that didn't succeed. Ask what might have been done to avoid the mistakes.
- Contribute your suggestions about how the matter could have been done more effectively.
- Ask what training or help you can provide.
- Agree on specific steps to be taken to ensure better results in the future.

[RESPONDING TO CRITICISM]

"Any fool can criticize, condemn and complain—
And most fools do."
—DALE CARNEGIE

It's one thing to think about how to manage conflict. It's quite another to ask the question, "Is it possible to benefit from criticism?" How we accept or reject criticism is more a matter of attitude than skill.

Consider the Source

You benefit most when you are able to evaluate the origin of a criticism. Is the person qualified in terms of knowledge, experience, or up-to-date information? Is the criticism comparable to previous ones? What does the record indicate? Has it happened before?

If so, is it likely to be even more valid now than it was before? Analyze the causes—who gains and who loses when you are criticized? Was it a consequence of another event? What event? Was the person criticizing you upset, ranting, and raving or cool, calm, and collected? If cool and calm, the criticism is probably more accurate. And you should probably respond more calmly yourself.

If you want to benefit from criticism, what do you do to put yourself on a course of recovery from attack? This question is especially valid for anyone in a position of leadership because vulnerability increases with exposure to mistakes, but it is useful for people who are not yet managers or upper executives. In these situations, how you recover from accusations or attack is more critical than the attack itself.

The hardcore issue is, are you resilient? Do you bounce back from adversity? People who have never held a management position sometimes envy those who do because of the rewards that usually accompany the role. But that view ignores the problems and difficulties.

Success depends to a great extent on how well unpleasant duties and responsibilities are met. Those who concentrate on the easy tasks and avoid the tougher, more unpleasant duties are asking for more trouble. The challenge is to maintain equilibrium in the process.

When you find yourself off-balance—stop! Pick your most critical problem. Give it your best analysis and try to do something about that one. When you've solved it or at least done everything possible you can, pick another and go to work on it. Carve the elephant up before you try to eat it.

Take up each problem as you get to it. Do the best you can. Tension and worrying drains our energy and accomplishes nothing.

You can actually benefit from criticism, after you recover from attack. Until you acknowledge the need to improve, there's little prospect it will happen. This is true for all of us.

In any organization there are bound to be differences of opinion. Managers who remember the people who disagreed with them and carry grudges become their own worst enemy.

Remember the warning: "Be careful about who you offend on your way up, you never know who will be your boss on the way down." Analyze why some people may feel cautious about you. Sometimes they will be watching your actions to see if you will ever support them.

Smart managers, whenever they have to oppose ideas, criticize someone, or track down responsibility for an error, will make a point of going one step further. They will try to heal the wound as quickly as possible. They will reassure people that their ideas and talents are still appreciated and that they are still considered valuable members of the team. It's childish to stop talking over something petty that should have been forgotten two seconds after it happened.

We often hold grudges because we don't know how to make amends. Pride gets in the way. We wait for the other person to make the first move. But a good manager will take that first step without waiting. They know it's their job to get disagreement out in the open and resolve it.

They help people forget mistakes. They realize that it benefits no one to let grudges sour working relationships because then everyone loses.

> *"Being defeated is often only a temporary condition.*
> *Giving up is what makes it permanent."*
> —MARILYN VOS SAVANT

React Constructively

Nobody likes to be criticized, but we all need it from time to time. Normally it is not the criticism itself that is disturbing but the manner in which it is given.

Optimists avoid feeling hurt, inadequate, or depressed. They have learned to accept criticism as a means of correcting errors and learning from them. The more tactful and constructive the criticism, the better the long-term results will be. You can't control the way your boss may criticize you, but you can control how you react to it.

Focus on the lessons to be learned, not the method. Keep in mind, a supervisor is measured by the success of his or her department. If you do not succeed, it will reflect on them as well.

[RESOLVING PROBLEMS]

"The most important thing to do in solving a problem is to begin."
—FRANK TYGER

When problems are not resolved, morale and productivity suffer. One (or more) of the following basic reasons usually plays a role. If you have unresolved problems in your workplace (and who does not?), you may find it useful to think about those that apply to your situation. Often, just being aware of the source of the problem can be the start of a process leading to its solution. A positive attitude and willingness to tackle these issues can only make the situation better.

- Associates often will not criticize supervisors.
- People tend to be self-protective of their positions in hopes for promotion.

- The presence of people with technical expertise tends to intimidate those who are afraid of admitting ignorance.

- A sense of urgency tends to stimulate unreliable judgments.

- Personal conflicts often work against constructive, cooperative problem solving.

- People see problems from their own viewpoint rather than a broader organizational perspective.

- Focusing on a distasteful situation clouds the atmosphere with tension, fear, and often uncertainty for all parties.

> *"A pessimist is one who makes difficulties*
> *of his opportunities and an optimist is one*
> *who makes opportunities of his difficulties."*
> —HARRY S. TRUMAN

CHAPTER 8

UPGRADING CAPABILITIES

> *"It is not because things are difficult that we do not dare,*
> *it is because we do not dare that they are difficult."*
> —SENECA

Capability is not the same as performance. The difference between competence (the *ability* to achieve) and the actual achievement or accomplishment itself is usually determined by the attitude we have toward the use or application of our ideas or skills. There is relationship between competence and performance, but only when competent people achieve goals. Competence without results is worthless.

How does competence increase or improve? It grows when people know what's expected of them; know what they expect of themselves; know their own limitations; know where to get help; can work with minimum direction; are able to measure their own performance against their own goals; and—most importantly—competence grows when people are comfortable with the idea that rewards will follow achievement, that people who accomplish the most should get the best rewards.

[FOSTER EMPLOYEE COMMITMENT]

Effective employees are not only competent to do the job, they must be committed to success and achieve the results expected. How can you foster commitment?

These practices are tried and true:

- Encourage minority opinions. To avoid deadening conformity, you may sometimes have to spark or prompt disagreement; if so, make sure that dissenting views are fully aired. Don't close a meeting quickly if everybody seems to agree.

- Reward innovation and creativity. When someone comes up with a novel and workable idea, applaud it. Spread the word that you appreciate it and you will encourage others to think creatively.

- Provide support for special circumstance conflicts. If people come to you with personal scheduling problems, cooperate to the extent that work allows.

- Whenever possible, give advance notice of schedule changes or overtime requirements. Indicate that you respect the fact that there are other demands on employees' time.

- Promote cooperation, not competition. One danger of overcommitment to an organization is that people become so caught up in their own agenda and ambitions they become single-minded. Discourage this by rewarding cooperation and cooperative approaches to problem solving. That's the essence of teamwork.

- Identify key people. The most frustrating situations managers face is losing the people who are most productive and committed. Know their personal goals.

Give them support and the opportunity to meet those goals. Your time and attention are critical.

* Keep your own organization commitment in focus. Your role model is unavoidable.

> *"Human beings can alter their lives by altering their attitudes of mind."*
> —WILLIAM JAMES

[HOW TO DISAGREE WITHOUT BEING DISAGREEABLE]

Frequently, disagreement is viewed as something to be avoided at all costs. There is nothing innately negative about disagreement, but your attitude can turn it into a major problem. Here's what can be done to convert controversy into positive results.

Remember the old slogan: "When two partners always agree, one of them is not necessary"? If there is some point you haven't thought about, be thankful if it is brought to your attention. Perhaps it will provide an opportunity to correct a potentially disastrous mistake.

Distrust your first instinctive impression. Our natural reaction in a disagreeable situation is to be defensive. Be careful—stay calm. Your first impulse may be you at your worst, not your best.

Control your temper. Be rational, not emotional, when dealing with personal problems or unsatisfactory performance.

Listen first. Give the other person a chance to talk. Let them finish. Do not resist, defend, or debate; this only raises barriers. Try to build bridges of understanding, not higher hurdles of mistrust.

Look for areas of agreement. When you have heard your opponent out, dwell first on these points and areas on which you agree.

Be honest. Look for points where you can admit error, then do it. Apologize for mistakes; it will help disarm opponents and reduce their defensiveness.

Promise to carefully study their ideas, and mean it. They may be right. It is easier at this stage to investigate early than to move rapidly ahead and find yourself in a position where others can say, "I tried to tell him, but he wouldn't listen."

Postpone action to allow time to think through the problem. Suggest that a new meeting be held later that day or soon thereafter, when all of the facts may be brought to bear. To prepare, write down the most difficult questions they have raised.

A good way to think about controversy is to ask yourself, "Could they be right or perhaps partly right? Is there truth or merit in their opposition or argument? Is my reaction one that will relieve the problem or will it just relieve my frustration? Will my reaction drive them further away or draw them closer? Will my reaction elevate the estimation good people have of me? Will I win or lose? What price will I have to pay if I win? If I'm quiet, will the disagreement blow over? Is this difficult situation an opportunity for me? What have I already learned from this?"

[BOUNCE BACK AND WIN]

"Adversity puts iron in your flesh."
—SOMERSET MAUGHAM

Longtime victory only comes to those who learn the most from losses. Nowhere is that more apparent than in professional sports, and nobody typifies that spirit more than quarterback Brett Favre.

In 1995, after being slammed to the ground countless times by defensive linemen, Favre became addicted to the painkiller Vicodin. He would take fifteen pills a night, and stop only two

days before a game. As soon as the game was over, he would return to the pills. Vomiting and not eating became a regular part
of his life. Pressured by his family and friends, he made a decision. He entered a rehabilitation program, where he stayed for
six weeks, and gave up alcohol as well as Vicodin.

Favre was named the NFL's Most Valuable Player a record
three consecutive years, 1995, 1996, and 1997. He also played
in 141 straight games—another record for NFL quarterbacks.
"I may get knocked down a lot . . . but I'll always get back up
again," he says.

Cartoonist Bill Mauldin was a smart aleck, rebellious kid who
was expelled from high school for his pranks. He loved to draw,
so to help his folks, at age thirteen, he borrowed twenty bucks
from his grandmother and took a course in cartooning. To get
experience, he illustrated anything from restaurant menus to po-
litical posters and gag cartoons. While in the Army in WWII, he
gave his superiors a hard time by creating the Willie and Joe cartoons. Soldiers loved its accuracy in portraying their plight. General Dwight Eisenhower overruled General George Patton who
wanted Mauldin's cartoons stopped. History judged Mauldin
wisely. He received two Pulitzer Prizes and was buried in Arling-
ton National Cemetery with a twenty-one gun salute.

[TEST NEW SKILLS]

Have you ever had an idea for a product, but shrugged it off,
thinking that if there was a market, someone else would already
have invented it? You may have given up a tremendous opportunity for success. For example:

Two Canadian journalists, Chris Haney and Scott Abbot,
seized their opportunity in the late 1970s. Because it had been
fifty years since the last successful board game was introduced,
most people thought they were a thing of the past.

Haney and Abbot ignored those doubts, spent five months developing a new board game, and introduced *Trivial Pursuit*.

At the Canadian Toy and Decoration Fair, only 200 of the games were sold. At the American International Toy Fair in New York City, only 144 orders were received. The box was too big. The game's design needed work. It cost too much.

But Haney and Abbot didn't give up. They sent their creation to as many newspapers and magazines as they could afford. They also sent it to a number of celebrities, most of who were mentioned in the questions they had written into the game. Johnny Carson talked about the game enthusiastically on *The Tonight Show* . . . and sales began to take off.

In 1984, twenty million games were sold in the United States alone.

> *"The gap between mediocrity and excellence is the difference measured by two things— indifference and determination."*

[DESERVE RESPECT]

Nobody believes it's better to work for a smart person who's emotionally unstable than for one who's steady. Studies from nearly 500 companies around the world have shown that 85 percent of what distinguishes an outstanding leader from an average one are qualities *other* than their technical expertise. The key factor has been identified as "emotional intelligence" or plain old compassion.

"Emotional intelligence" is composed of both personal and social competence.

Those with personal competence are self-aware. If they are able to read their emotions, assess their strengths and limits, and act in a self-confident way. Their emotional intelligence is high. They are able to manage themselves well. They're in control.

Social competence suggests a person who is quite sensitive to the inner world of others. They are socially aware. They are empathic. They realize that when pride becomes arrogance, followers disappear.

Successful leaders know how to manage relationships. Are you an influential motivator and catalyst for change? Do you build others up, create a web of relationships, and work well with teams? If so, you're demonstrating a high level of emotional intelligence and will deserve respect.

Can you keep destructive emotions in check? Are you trustworthy and flexible? Are you driven to improve performance, ready to act when needed, and optimistic in the face of difficulties? If so, you have the capability to become a successful leader.

[BE A COACH]

"What I need is someone who will make me do what I am capable of doing."
—RALPH WALDO EMERSON

Fortunately, coaching and training can improve attitudes. Managers are the key. Indeed, those who fail to be coaches and trainers limit their own future as well as retard the growth of their team.

Coaching puts those who supervise in a special position to convert affirmative attitudes into on-the-job improvements. It's a continuing process. After each achievement, new goals should be set and then the process starts over again.

Franklin C. Ashby and Arthur R. Pell, in their book *Embracing Excellence*, point out ten areas where coaching is most needed:

1. *Management:* Assuring that assignments are clearly presented, holding employees accountable, providing

direction and support, facilitating consensus, and providing mentoring, trust, recognition, and rewards.

2. *Empathic Listening:* Talking less and paying more attention when others talk. In addition, asking the right questions, not interrupting, showing enthusiasm, balancing seriousness with humor, and good body language.

3. *Collaboration:* Developing relationships with associates within and outside of the department, team, or work group, treating people consistently, building alliances, networking, maintaining a win–win attitude, and mingling with others.

4. *Conflict Resolution:* Developing constructive approaches to confronting others as conflicts arise, and giving clear, direct feedback in a nonaggressive way to demonstrate respect and support.

5. *Positive Attitudes:* Giving consideration to other view-points with an open mind, demonstrating enthusiasm, focusing on positive solutions rather than negative problems, and presenting opposing views with a win–win approach.

6. *Self-Confidence*: Being willing to take reasonable risks without becoming defensive or overwhelmed by fear of failing, and taking tough stands in a decisive, forceful way.

7   *Being Respectful:* Letting others know that they can make a valuable contribution, demonstrating a true respect for different viewpoints without appearing to be condescending or arrogant.

8. *Strategic Leadership:* Viewing the business from a big-picture, long-term perspective, articulating ways to implement plans, and developing needed initiatives.

9. *Establishing Priorities:* Managing time effectively, setting reasonable standards, letting others know what is expected of them, and holding them accountable without overmanaging.

10. *Upward Communication:* Keeping upper managers advised, knowing their priorities, selling your concepts, promoting the accomplishments of all members of your team.

As a coach, a manager can check on an employee's understanding of what has been learned; see how effectively work has been done; point out changes; demonstrate how best to handle specific duties. It's good to remember that coaches never achieve perfection in others or themselves.

Effective coaching permits a manager to focus attention on those aspects of an individual's performance requiring improvement; evaluate attitudes, skills, knowledge, and aptitudes; hold each person accountable for specific responsibilities; and, above all, give credit where credit is due.

The best coaches succeed by influencing employees with their positive attitudes and not dominating them. Effective managers establish authority by demonstrating knowledge and experience. Having a thorough knowledge of an individual's job is impressive in itself, but it also stimulates others to consider your suggestions or recommendations more carefully. To make your coaching sessions pay off, here's how to begin:

1. Review background reports maintained on the employee. What is the evidence of:
   - Their progress, or lack of it?
   - Their specific skills?
   - Their ability to lead?

2. Determine the major job responsibilities now required.

3. Analyze results achieved.

4. Evaluate the quality and extent of training received. How has it been applied?

During the coaching sessions:

*   Explain that the purpose of coaching is to help them perform at their best.
*   Detail the steps involved, sequence, and schedule.
*   Invite questions and respond to them.
*   Clarify results expected.

When discussing areas where improvement may be needed:

*   Concentrate on only one or two major areas at a time.
*   Steer in the direction of self-criticism. Ask questions, such as: "What did you see in this situation that you haven't encountered before?" or, "What choice would have been better, and why?"
*   Observe more than you talk; you'll learn more.

Always be sure to record what you've seen and heard. Jot down specific areas to be covered during future sessions, including:

*   Previous results.
*   Objectives to be achieved.
*   Be sure to give advance notice of meetings with an agenda and time needed.

Best results are achieved via continuing contact using these seven techniques:

1. Note and commend progress.

2. Define problems clearly.

3. Do not overlook difficulties.

4. Offer assistance on a continuing basis.

5. Commit to improvement with written goals.

6. Identify specific training needs.

7. In a competitive situation, let people know where they stand in relation to others.

Employees who are well coached usually feel better about their jobs. They tend to do their best because they know someone in authority has an intense personal interest in their performance and in their success.

Here's a great example of a situation where people have learned to accept the value of each other's coaching, as reported in *Inc. Magazine*. Bob Metcalf started a company called Three Com Corporation. Because he realized his own limitations as a manager, he recognized the need to bring in a professional, experienced manager to take charge of the duties where he was not effective.

He hired Bill Kroust, realizing they both had much to learn from this collaboration. Metcalf had an academic background, where the goal was to win the argument. Kroust came from a world where the goal was to "get the order," so he taught him how to sell.

Kroust also taught Metcalf the value of planning, how to resolve emotional issues, and how to avoid abrasive situations.

But this was not a one-way street. Metcalf taught Kroust how to be a better public speaker, how to avoid trivia, and the value of principles and integrity. He taught him to provide enough opportunity for people to take risks, even when they fail. In addition, he learned how to lighten up. How to laugh at himself and see the humor in situations. They did not agree on many issues, but by working together, both are stronger and the company is, too.

The benefits of coaching are available at all levels of an organization. Seek out opportunities to coach and be coached.

CHAPTER 9

CONQUERING BURNOUT AND STRESS

*"Expect trouble as an inevitable part of life and when it comes,
hold your head high, look it squarely in the eye and say,
'I will be bigger than you. You cannot defeat me.'"*
—ANN LANDERS

All jobs have their share of stress. If they didn't, they would quickly become boring. It's when *stress* becomes *distress* that problems occur. The stress may show up in the way our behavior has changed. People who had always been patient become impatient. Calm people may become tense. Employees, who before were always cooperative, rebel. Others may show physical symptoms or complain that they have trouble falling asleep or in sleeping through the night. They're often tired all the time—even if they do get a good rest. They may have stomach pains, a fast heartbeat, or frequent headaches.

Rest can cure physical fatigue, but some people are more likely to feel mentally drained on the job. If they work with computers, for example, remind them that physical exercise can help. Suggest that they take a lunchtime walk, go swimming or jogging, or participate in a sport after work. Many companies now have exercise rooms in which employees can use a stationary bike or a weight machine during their lunch hour. Those who have a regular regimen are less likely to become mentally fatigued.

> "*You cannot tailor-make the situations in life, but you can tailor-make the attitudes to fit those situations before they arise.*"
> —ZIG ZIGLAR

[BURNOUT]

People are not light bulbs. A light bulb shines brightly, then suddenly—poof! It burns out. People burn out slowly and often imperceptibly. Although some burnouts result in physical breakdowns such as a heart attack or ulcers, most are psychological. People lose enthusiasm, energy, and motivation, and it shows up in many ways. They hate their job, can't stand coworkers, distrust the team leader, and dread coming to work each morning.

Burnout results from too much stress, but that's not the only cause. Others include frustration over unmet promises or being passed over for an expected promotion or salary increase. Some managers burn out because of the pressures of having to make decisions that can cause catastrophic problems. Others fade from excessively long hours or unrewarding work. People with positive attitudes are much better candidates to avoid these problems.

Burnout is easier to identify than to cure. The telltale signs include less assertiveness and acceptance of mediocrity; the drive to improve slackens, productivity falls off, and relationships turn sour. These suggestions will help you put the brakes on a slide into the doldrums.

[TEST YOUR STRESS LEVEL]

Take this quiz to see how close you are to having serious stress problems.

In the box in front of each question, mark "SA" for Strongly Affirmative, "A" for Affirmative, "N" for Negative, and "SN" for Strongly Negative.

1._____ Are you fatigued throughout the day?

2._____ Do you speak up less often in business meetings than you previously did?

3._____ Are you forgetting things more frequently?

4._____ Are you tired, even after a good night's sleep?

5._____ Does your mind rarely seem in full gear?

6._____ Do you seem further behind at the end of the day than when you started?

7._____ Are you less patient with others?

8._____ Do you spend less time on hobbies?

9._____ Are accomplishments seldom pleasing to you?

10._____ Do you rarely operate at full speed during waking hours?

Score ten points if the answer is Strong Affirmative (SA), seven points for an Affirmative (A), three points for a Negative (N), and no points for a Strong Negative (SN).

Evaluate your score. Zero to 15 points indicates you are either totally inactive or have your act together; 16 to 50 shows you are unlikely to suffer from burnout; 51 to 80 indicates you are on thin ice, burnout could be close; 86 to 100 means you are a walking stress bomb.

[MANAGING STRESS]

When stress on the job is high, steps must be taken to manage it. Some physicians suggest tranquilizers and other medication. But you can manage your own stress if you:

- Keep in tiptop shape. Watch your diet and engage in a regular exercise program.

- Learn to relax. Participate in programmed relaxation exercises. Be sure to reserve time to spend alone.

- Learn to respect yourself. People with high self-esteem are less likely to be adversely affected by pressure from others.

- Acknowledge your inability to please everyone, all the time.

- Keep learning. The experience of ongoing learning keeps you alert, open-minded, and stimulated.

- Develop a support team. Avoid major stress by having friends and family members available to back you up when things don't go well.

- Accept only commitments that are important to you. Politely turn down projects that will drain your time and energy.

- Seek new ways of using your creativity. By rethinking the way you perform routine tasks and developing creative approaches to new assignments, you can make them less stressful to handle.

- Welcome changes. Consider changes as new challenges rather than threats.

- Replace negative images in your mind with positive ones. There's proof that there is power in positive thinking.

- If your hobby or leisure activity makes you even more tense (e.g., competitive sports or Tournament Bridge), drop it. Substitute one that is truly relaxing.
- Give yourself permission to have a life. Enjoy activities with family and friends. Don't feel guilty when you're not thinking about your job.

> *"Adopting the right attitude can convert a negative stress into a positive one."*
> —HANS SELYE

[COPING WITH BURNOUT]

Recovery from burnout requires honest examination of these basic issues:

- Divergent goals. The firm's interests and yours do not coincide. You are moving in different directions. You may come to feel that room for professional growth and upward mobility are severely limited.
- Boring and unchallenging work. Too much routine, few opportunities for exploration. Repetition prevails.
- Not enough responsibility and influence. New challenges or increases in authority are scarce.
- Changes in personal objectives. Family needs may emerge that put career considerations on hold. Health problems may become prominent.
- New educational or technical requirements. They can put a high achiever at risk unless anticipated and time is allocated for completion.
- Maximum effort results in minimum recognition. When you are usually selected to do the tough jobs,

but praise, compensation, and promotions are lacking, take these steps:

1. Document what has happened.
2. Check your personal objectives.
3. Request a meeting to discuss why you are being taken for granted. This could be a key step in your growth, but it may not be if you wait for someone else to initiate action.

[RELIEVING STRESS AT THE OFFICE]

People react differently to stress. What works for some may not work for others. The approaches that follow can all yield significant benefits during your workday:

Take a Break

When Charley feels undue pressure, he tries to remove himself from the scene for a short time. He leaves his desk, puts on his coat, and goes out of the building. A short walk around the block or parking lot for ten minutes renews him and restores his perspective.

Esther works in the downtown section of her city. When she feels stressed, she also leaves the building and relaxes by window shopping in a nearby mall.

Stan's boss does not approve of people leaving the building during working hours. So, when he's stressed, he finds an errand to do in another department. Removing himself from the place of stress gives his mind an opportunity to refocus. A change of scenery helps alleviate tension.

Exercise

If you work in a room with twenty other people, it's not a good idea to do jumping jacks in the middle of the floor. But many exercises are unobtrusive. Breathing exercises are easy to do and don't disturb other people. Inhale deeply through your nose and let the air out slowly though your mouth. Do this several times. You'll notice how your entire body reacts and begins to relax.

Ted's company has a well-equipped gym. When under pressure, he goes there, gets on a stationary bike, and pumps for five or ten minutes—not enough to work up a sweat, but just right to relieve his tension.

Change Tasks

In most jobs people have several projects or phases of projects they are working on at any one time. If pressure becomes too great on the current activity, shift to another for a while. Heather was so concerned about meeting a deadline she couldn't concentrate on her work. She caught herself making stupid errors and poor judgments so she put the project aside and worked on another assignment for a half hour. When she returned to her priority, her mind was clear.

Talk to a Friend

For some, the best way to relieve stress is to discuss it with a friend. Peter phones a good friend to talk out the problem. Although he doesn't expect his friend to solve it for him, verbalizing what is on his mind to another person helps clear the picture for him. In addition, sometimes a few minutes of chit-chat can reduce tension.

Find Your Own Solution

Many other tension-relievers can be effective. One man reported that when he is stressed, he goes out to his car, closes the windows—and screams.

Dierdre, who fortunately has a private office, reported that her tension relief came in performing yoga for a few minutes.

Jim goes (only in his mind, unfortunately) to the stream near his summer cottage and listens to the water burbling over the rocks.

Others find help in meditation or prayer.

Any one of these techniques—or others that you develop—can help you reduce stress in the workplace.

> *"Holding on the anger is like grasping a hot coal*
> *with the intent of throwing it at someone else—*
> *you are the one who gets burned.*
> —BUDDHA

[USING YOUR POSITIVE ATTITUDE TO HELP OTHERS]

Your own positive attitude can help put a burned-out member of your staff on the road to recovery in these ways:

- Be supportive. Demonstrate sincere interest by encouraging discussion of concerns and helping to make adjustments.

- Consider changing job functions. Assigning different activities and responsibilities or transferring to another team can change the climate and provide new outlets to restart.

- Provide an opportunity to acquire new skills. This not only helps focus on learning, but can also increase value for the company.

- If, despite your efforts, there is no progress, strongly suggest professional counseling.

Knowing your behavioral tendencies is not enough. They are a signal to take steps to change your attitude. By reviewing the information in this book and applying it, you can reduce your susceptibility to stress and burnout. You can change your life by converting negative thinking to positive thinking—and positive actions. It's not easy, but it's well worth the effort.

"To be calm when others are not shifts the
advantage to you in two ways:
—It stabilizes your position.
—It encourages allies impressed by your self-control."

CHAPTER 10

POSITIVE ATTITUDE—
THE KEY TO SUCCESS

*"Things turn out best for the people who make
the best of the way things turn out."*
JOHN WOODEN

As you review your approach to your life and job, you realize that a positive attitude not only influences your successes; it is a powerful factor in avoiding burnout and keeping your skills up to date. A positive attitude creates the climate for success and sets the stage for potential winners to actually win.

A positive attitude prompts success. We are successful when we genuinely appreciate what we have, and do not allow ourselves to be depressed because of what we don't have. Put simply, attitude provides the urge to succeed whether in serving on a committee or seeking a position of power in a multinational corporation. It may be the drive to achieve success in business, serve humankind in one of the professions, or add something to the beauty of life through one of the arts.

The key to success is working persistently toward specific objectives under your own power. When necessary, you prove that you can count on nobody but yourself. Success means progressing from what is acceptable to what is excellent. It seldom comes easy.

Excellence is usually the result of a long, tough apprenticeship. To increase the odds that hard work achieves your goals, these personal attributes are essential:

- *Self-esteem.* Unless you regard yourself as a valuable individual, a worthy and capable human being, there's little chance you'll be able to change or control the conditions and opportunities presented.

- *Responsibility.* You hold yourself strictly accountable for what happens in your life. You willingly assume full responsibility for the events that result in either success or failure.

- *Optimism.* To be successful, you must understand clearly that there are situations beyond the scope of your capabilities—but not expect defeat. Those who are successful feel good about themselves, have confidence in the future, and work productively in the present.

- *Steady Progress.* Measure success step by step. Success-oriented individuals keep their goals before them constantly. Not only do goals measure progress, but they also serve to motivate and direct future behavior.

- *Imagination.* Without imagination you can't visualize what it might be like to experience exciting new and beneficial ventures before they occur. Successful people use their imaginations constantly and creatively, testing ideas in the light of possibilities.

- *Awareness.* You must always be aware of what is going on around you. People succeed because they are curious. Their eyes are always open to new opportunities.

- *Creativity.* Loosen up. Think out of the box. Successful people make a habit of looking at problems, situations, and opportunities from different vantage points. They constantly ask, "Why is this so? What makes it different? When did it happen? Who will benefit most from change or a new direction?"

> *"Always bear in mind that your own resolution to succeed is more important than any other one thing."*
> —ABRAHAM LINCOLN

[CRITERIA FOR SUCCESSFUL LEADERS]

Avoiding failure is not the same as achieving success. Lee Iacocca is a living example of a leader whose positive attitude enabled him to accept the risk of failure when he took on the job as head of Chrysler Motors. In interviews, during discussions, even in television commercials for his company, Iacocca reflected a toughness of purpose and a driving determination to win. He's a "Let's tell it like it is and get on with it" type of executive. These are the same qualities he sought in the men and women he hired to fill top posts at Chrysler. Those who turn out best, in Iacocca's candid and often colorful opinion, could be described in these ways:

- *Risk-Taking Mavericks:* They are cool, calculating risk-takers who will lay their jobs on the line if necessary to get a new, untested, but important project underway.

- *Controlled Workaholics:* The eight-hour day for these people is the exception rather than the routine. They find their jobs so exciting and challenging, that actual time at work holds little interest or meaning for them.

Accomplishment is the compensation that satisfies them most.

- *Honest Communicators:* They speak out bravely, even at the risk of being blunt. What they are committed to achieve is stated in a way that stimulates their listeners to action. They create a climate in which two-way communication is encouraged. The ideas they express are clear. Factual feedback follows.

- *Fearless Delegators:* They have no fear of delegating important tasks to others. Team members get the chance to succeed or fail on their own. They motivate by example so people are encouraged to do their best.

- *Practical Planners:* They have the foresight to see the task in total, rather than attempting to handle important jobs in bits and pieces. They force themselves to think ahead, set priorities, and measure progress as accurately as possible.

- *Tough-Minded Decision-Makers:* They don't hesitate if it means dropping a favorite program that is no longer valuable. Veteran employees who are not effective are replaced, however painful the departure may be.

- *Dreamers with Common Sense:* Dreamers are tolerated if there are concrete results within a reasonable time. Performance is the measure used, not expectations.

- *Sacrificial Performers:* They willingly do more than expected. When they get excited, they generate excitement in others. They look forward to their work. They cooperate and interact, but don't pout. Their energy output is directed and controlled. They have the willpower to keep going despite a lack of encouragement once they know they're on the right track.

[THE ATTRIBUTES OF WINNERS]

Winners recognize the importance of four vital principles in their relationships:

The first is *everyone can be motivated in some way*. If we accept the notion that this person or that person simply can't ever be motivated, they won't. This means that managers must find out what those motivation keys are very early on in the relationship.

The second is *people tend to do things for* their *reasons, not yours*. The challenge is to find their reasons so they can be applied at work. Only then can you address their problems and make sure their concerns are taken into account in terms of the tasks to be done.

The third is *overextension of a strength can become a weakness*. I'll never forget this example:

My client, Carl Adams, was the president of an organization. He was so obsessed with promptness that he always arrived way ahead of time. He believed that people who were early, like himself, were bound to make the most valuable contributions. It got to the point where the earlier an employee arrived at a meeting, the more legitimate Adams would consider their contribution to be. It had nothing at all to do with the value of the recommendation but was solely based on his obsession with being on time. Promptness is a fine trait, but if you carry it so far that it prevails over the content of what people have to say, you're going make some serious mistakes.

The fourth is *you do not motivate people; you create an environment in which they will be self-motivated*. That's the challenge for all leaders. If you're trying to continuously find bigger, better, and tastier carrots to dangle in front of people, you'll soon run out of carrots. If people are going to get along without your direct supervision, without you constantly telling them what to do, they must be encouraged to take action themselves.

[ENTHUSIASM IS CONTAGIOUS]

Enthusiasm is the most obvious and visible evidence of a positive attitude.

Tommy Lasorda, the longtime manager of the Los Angeles Dodgers and one of the most upbeat people in professional sports, is convinced his attitude is contagious. "When I come into this clubhouse" he says, "if I'm dejected, depressed, and tired and the players see me that way, what's the attitude and the atmosphere going to be? If I walk in full of enthusiasm, full of self-confidence and proud to be putting on that uniform, all of those things are also contagious. That's the attitude this team will have." It's the same with executives or other leaders. If they walk into the office or factory in a bad mood, dejection spreads quickly. On the other hand, if they walk in full of enthusiasm, optimism, and confidence, that positive attitude will spread to everyone.

Lasorda also has some very definite views on the relationship between attitude and loyalty, and how to keep it alive. He believes, "Loyalty means you give in return what is given to you—that's how you get good performance, and that's how you win. If you love your work, you will take pride in it. How many people," he asks, "are walking the streets of this great nation who can honesty and truthfully say they would love to work for their organizations when they're dead and gone?"

You are as young as your faith
As old as your doubts
As young as your self confidence
As old as your fears
As young as your hope
As old as your despair.
Years may wrinkle the skin
But to give up enthusiasm
Wrinkles the soul."
                                    —SAMUEL ULLMAN

Effective leaders understand how attitude influences behavior and use that knowledge to move organizations forward. The bottom line is to act in ways that are mutually beneficial:

- When you help people be successful, most of them will be inclined to help you. If you set up roadblocks, they will retaliate whenever they can.

- If you earn respect, you will have few problems and less hostility.

- Humiliating assignments or directives will almost always boomerang and be repaid at the worst possible time.

- Favor most those who get the best results, not the ones who always say what they think you want to hear.

- Don't expect to be popular—look for respect, not gratitude.

- Deliver on commitments, don't overpromise, and get participation in goal-setting.

[THE HAZARDS OF SUCCESS]

Whoever said that the two hardest things to handle in life are failure and success was very wise. That's why real winners always turn to the next challenge. The key is to learn how to learn, and then learn more. Problems arise when people assume success is inevitable. A positive attitude supports confidence that when circumstances are out of your control, you will be able to adapt and prevail.

There are patterns revealing why some people lose more consistently than others. Some people, when opportunity knocks, are out in the backyard looking for four-leaf clovers. They don't know opportunity when they see it. They don't learn from their mistakes. Their objectives are unclear to them, so they're bound to be unclear to other people. They're inconsistent. They don't pursue a steady course toward goals.

They don't have strong allies, so they can't draw upon help when they need it. They overemphasize money or status. They resist change; they're not adaptable. They're not resilient; they haven't learned how to bounce back. And they don't capitalize on their own strengths so the impact of their weaknesses is much more serious than it needs to be.

The life lesson is, *don't take your attitude for granted at anytime, at any age, in any place.* That's why winners win, and losers lose. Attitude truly makes the difference. We are all surrounded by evidence of this fact every day. What you make of it is up to you.

Do you wish for greater acceptance?
Think Positively to brighten personality.
Do you wish to be more successful?
Think Positively to develop your career.
Do you wish to have more ability?
Think Positively to improve your skills.
Do you wish to be happier?
Think Positively to improve your judgments.
Do you wish your life to be better tomorrow?
Think Positive thoughts today.

> **"***Attitude is the scale on which we balance our strengths and limitations. Outside circumstances are less important in the long run than our inner view of our selves.***"**